BOOK #3 IN THE MYSTIC'S GIFT/ROYCE HOLLOWAY SERIES

THE TREASURE IN ANTIGUA

SKIP JOHNSON

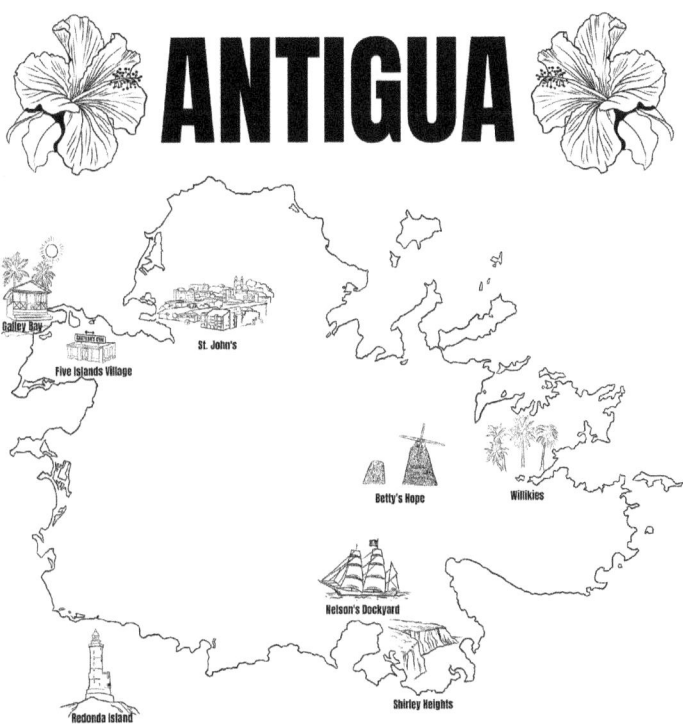

Copyright © 2022 Skip Johnson

All rights reserved. No part of this book may be reproduced or transmitted in any form or by any means, electronic or mechanical, including photocopying, recording, or by any information storage and retrieval system without written permission of the publisher, except for the inclusion of brief quotations in a review.

Cover and Interior Design by Dino Marino | dinomarino.com
Copy Editing by Robin Fuller
Proofreading by Linda Dutro
Paperback ISBN: 978-1-7352511-8-9
eBook ISBN: 978-1-7352511-7-2

"Could a greater miracle occur than for us to look through each other's eyes for an instant?"

–Henry David Thoreau

OTHER BOOKS BY SKIP JOHNSON

SEE ALL BOOKS AT WWW.SKIPJOHNSONAUTHOR.COM

THE STATUE'S SECRET

Prominent Newport lawyer David Langley is a tormented man consumed by anxiety, guilt, and regret as his world falls apart more and more each day.

Until . . .

He fortuitously comes across an ancient Caribbean statue, which is soon verified as one of the most magnificent, sacred artifacts ever unearthed.

One with a unique blessing bestowed upon it for the benefit of its fourteenth century owner—and for all future owners . . .

A blessing that it seems could finally lead David on a path to a transformed life.

That is, *if* David can find his way to a mystical meeting with three wise, carefully chosen mentors at a remote location deep within the Dominican Republic jungle . . . within 48 hours.

Otherwise, the statue and its remarkable gift will vanish forever.

As David frantically, desperately makes his way to his final Dominican destination and the opportunity for an inspired new life, you'll find yourself enthusiastically cheering him on every step of the way.

Then, at some point you may realize the one who is truly on the journey . . . is *you*.

THE LOTTERY WINNER'S GREATEST RIDE

When Phillip Westford won the biggest lottery in history, he never dreamed there would be a price to pay.

A very *large* price that would shake his world to the core . . .

But just when he is at his breaking point, Phillip meets a mysterious old Irishman named Patrick O'Rourke who claims he knows the secret for getting the distraught young man back to happiness.

That is, *if* Phillip is willing to undertake a trek to find three wise mentors across the globe.

Join Phillip on a magnificent train ride as he shares the inspiring, incredible story of his journey of transformation with Juliette McKelvey—a young journalist who is on her own desperate journey to rebuild her crumbling life.

It's a ride to happiness you'll soon realize . . . you were *destined* to be on.

THE GENTLEMAN'S JOURNEY:
A HEARTWARMING STORY OF COURAGE, COMPASSION, AND WISDOM

(Book 2 in The Mystic's Gift/Royce Holloway series)

Five years after that glorious week when Maya shared six life-changing principles from an ancient secret book of wisdom with him, Royce is ready for a new chapter—to push his skills and his life to a higher level and make an even greater impact on the world.

In fact, he feels something is *leading* him to do that very thing. . .

So much so, that when Royce's journey takes him to the spectacular, historical Jekyll Island Club Hotel on the Georgia coast, it doesn't surprise him one bit when he "coincidentally" meets a mysterious, well-seasoned world traveler, a traveler whose life was *destined* to intersect with Royce Holloway's—in an unforgettable way for them both.

Join Royce on this powerful, spellbinding trek full of mystics, miracles, and inspirational stories.

You may find *your* life will never be the same again. . .

THE MYSTIC'S GIFT:
A STORY ABOUT LOSS, LETTING GO . . . AND LEARNING TO SOAR

(Book 1 in The Mystic's Gift/Royce Holloway series)

A spellbinding, deeply moving story that is quickly becoming a self-help classic. Following a sudden, unimaginable personal tragedy at a point in his midlife where Royce Holloway thought he had it all, he is introduced to a wise, exotic, enchanting mentor named Maya, who takes Royce on a powerful journey of courageous self-discovery and incredible possibilities.

What he learns on this captivating, often poignant trek across two continents will change him in a powerful way, but you may find that the life changed most . . . is yours.

HIDDEN JEWELS OF HAPPINESS:
POWERFUL ESSAYS FOR FINDING AND SAVORING THE GIFTS ON YOUR JOURNEY

A book of wisdom, encouragement, and empowerment for dealing with life's daily challenges. Let Skip reveal to you the seemingly hidden gifts that are all around us, waiting to be discovered and enjoyed. You'll feel inspired, enlightened, and happier with every page.

GRATEFUL FOR EVERYTHING:
LEARNING, LIVING, AND LOVING THE GREAT GAME OF LIFE

A deeply engaging book which provides a blueprint for using the power of gratitude to increase your happiness and fulfillment. You'll find delightful stories and practical ideas for turning your life into a great game to play each day, instead of a dreary battle to be fought.

DEDICATION

To Anne Marie

Each memory of our time in Antigua
is like a soft breeze from the island,
whispering a gentle reminder
of the treasure you are in my life.

TABLE OF CONTENTS

CHAPTER 1 1

CHAPTER 2 7

CHAPTER 3 14

CHAPTER 4 17

CHAPTER 5 24

CHAPTER 6 28

CHAPTER 7 38

CHAPTER 8 49

CHAPTER 9 52

CHAPTER 10 60

CHAPTER 11	69
CHAPTER 12	82
CHAPTER 13	91
CHAPTER 14	100
CHAPTER 15	107
CHAPTER 16	121
ABOUT SKIP JOHNSON	135
CAN I ASK A FAVOR?	137

CHAPTER 1

Stepping out of the airport into the sweltering tropical heat, Royce Holloway couldn't help but smile as he quietly said to himself, *I promise I'll never complain about the summer temperatures in Atlanta again!*

But the heat was forgotten as he scanned the area, quickly caught up in the beauty of his surroundings: majestic, towering palm trees swaying in the soft, moist Caribbean breeze; groves of hibiscus, laden with their trumpet-shaped red flowers; and in the distance, a long stretch of rocky hills framing the entire scene like a colorful, mesmerizing Gauguin painting.

It had only been five hours since his flight left Jacksonville, but during that time, Royce had been consumed with thinking about what all had happened during his short stay on Jekyll Island. The time he had spent with Godfrey Tillman still felt surreal. Having the opportunity to share an evening of conversation with a person who'd had such an impact on so many peoples' lives was priceless—and Royce did not take one minute of that conversation for granted.

But now, in what seemed like the blink of an eye, Godfrey was gone, and after a two-day weather delay in leaving Jekyll due to flight cancellations, Royce Holloway was now a world away, on the magnificent island of Antigua.

Looking back, although it all still seemed so strange, he knew those lessons were exactly what he had needed to learn.

Royce had gone to Jekyll because he somehow felt *led* to be there, odd as that might sound. However, that is exactly what had happened: he was led by something bigger than himself. After all those powerful days in the gardens with his wonderful Indian mentor Maya five years ago, Royce's life had certainly changed. He began living his life at a new level, watching his world turn into something that he never could have imagined. His spiritual and personal life had grown unfathomably powerful, and all those around him were empowered by his presence, too.

But then, after five years, Royce had felt himself desperately wanting to raise the bar of his personal growth even more. So, off to Jekyll he had gone, to one of his all-time favorite hotels. And there—at the hotel bar, of all places—he fortuitously met the jovial, wise Englishman Godfrey Tillman, and they spent an incredible afternoon and night together, in the midst of a raging hurricane! Godfrey, it turned out, was *also* led to be at Jekyll. As a former leader under Mahatma Gandhi and a powerfully spiritual part of the nonresistance movement against the British, Godfrey had been one of the original owners of a copy of *The Six Principles of Sacred Power*. Then, as the last of the original book owners, he had traveled to Jekyll to meet

Royce—unbeknownst to him—and teach him the secretive Four Daily Pillars of Wisdom. These pillars were only allowed to be passed on to those who had been blessed with a copy of *The Six Principles*. At the five-year mark, book owners—including Royce—were allowed to participate in the sacred process of learning the Four Pillars from a senior leader in the movement.

Godfrey had been Royce's mentor that ethereal night at Jekyll.

Not only that, but Godfrey had been personally charged by Maya to make sure Royce learned the lessons as effectively and efficiently as possible. The Four Pillars were essentially a "booster shot" of wisdom that book owners would recite each morning to make sure the message of *The Six Principles of Sacred Power* stayed fresh in their minds.

Shortly after their lessons that night on Jekyll had finished, Godfrey had tragically died—a source of much grief for Royce. But just before his death, Godfrey had given Royce his special ruby ring—evidence of his successful completion of the instruction on the Four Pillars.

Godfrey had one final request: he wanted Royce to go to Antigua—Godfrey's island of residence and place of refuge over the last many years. There, Godfrey assured him, Royce would find someone he needed to meet. Although Godfrey wouldn't say whom, he reminded Royce to be patient and allow his impending future in the Caribbean to unfold—as he had been taught by *The Six Principles of Sacred Power*. To provide him with a contact on the island, Godfrey shared with

Royce the phone number of his Antiguan housekeeper, Suzanne Dismont, a long-time trusted part of Godfrey's life. While still at the Jekyll hotel shortly after Godfrey's passing, Royce had called Suzanne and told her he was headed to Antigua to fulfill the Englishman's last wish. Suzanne responded as if she knew exactly what Royce meant—almost as if it had all been choreographed. She then instructed a driver to meet Royce at the hotel and drive him to the airport, so Royce could begin his new adventure.

Now, two days later, as Royce stood outside the small but beautiful airport upon arriving in Antigua, taking it all in, his reverie was suddenly interrupted by a woman calling his name.

"Mr. Holloway! Mr. Holloway, over here!"

About twenty yards ahead to his left, Royce saw that the voice was coming from a woman in the fourth vehicle in line—an open-air jeep. The woman had beautiful brown skin and a big smile, and she appeared to be in her early forties. As Royce walked toward her with his luggage, she offered in a friendly Caribbean accent, "I'm Suzanne Dismont. Come on, jump in."

Throwing his suitcase in the back of the jeep, Royce slid into the passenger seat next to Suzanne.

Hmmm, thought Royce uncertainly. He had pictured Godfrey's housekeeper as someone a little . . . older. To his surprise, Suzanne was an attractive woman who seemed to possess a radiant personality and a free spirit. "Well, I have to say, I kind of thought you would be a little more, um. . ."

Suzanne interrupted him. "Housekeeper-ish, maybe?"

"Oh, no, no . . . that's not what I meant at all. I just thought when Godfrey told me you had been with him a long time, you know, you'd be. . ."

Chuckling, she raised her hand as if to stop him. "Mr. Holloway, I'm Suzanne, 'the old, frumpy housekeeper.' "

Embarrassed, Royce smiled back at her and added, "Ok, ok, let's start over: hi, I'm Royce! By the way, I'm not 'Mr. Holloway.' That's my dad."

Suzanne smiled broadly. "Touché, Royce. Welcome to the island! I'm so glad you're here." Her countenance softened and she added, "I am sad it's under these circumstances, but I'll tell you that Mr. Tillman would not want this to be a solemn occasion. He would want your time here to be a joyous one, and he would want his life to be celebrated, not mourned."

"Well," said Royce, "if it were me, I think I would be the same way. Incidentally," he added with a puzzled look, "I'm not exactly sure *why* I'm here. Could you shed some light on that for me?"

"Don't worry, there's plenty of time to find out about all that. Trust me, there will be a lot to learn while you're here. For now, let's drive up to Mr. Tillman's home. It's about thirty minutes from here, and you'll get to see some stellar parts of Antigua along the way."

Royce crinkled his forehead. "Wait . . . did you say 'an-TEE-guh'?"

Suzanne threw back her head and laughed. "Royce, now that you're here, you simply *must* learn how to properly pronounce the name of our island."

Royce laughed, too. "Guess you're right! Otherwise, they may know I'm not a local. Not that this pale skin of mine would give it away or anything..."

Suzanne grinned.

"So, I've always pronounced it 'an-TEE-gwa.' In fact, that's the way Godfrey pronounced it, too," he protested.

"Of course. Most Americans pronounce it that way. Whenever Mr. Tillman went to the States, he decided it wasn't worth the resistance, so he always pronounced it like the Americans do. But I assure you, it's 'an-TEE-guh.'"

"Got it," Royce said with a sarcastic salute. "See what a great student I am?"

"We'll see," said Suzanne, with a playfully doubting smile. "Now buckle up, the roads will be a little bumpy along the way."

Royce obliged, then as Suzanne pressed the gas, the car swerved around the others in front of it, heading out of the airport and up island to what had been the home of Godfrey Tillman.

CHAPTER 2

Suzanne reached into her purse and grabbed a rectangular item about the size of a small brick, neatly wrapped in aluminum foil. She tossed it to Royce, who reached out and grabbed the item with a look of surprise.

"Don't worry, it's not ticking," she said with a laugh.

"What is it?"

"Banana bread. It's a staple around here, and I thought you might be hungry after your flight." She smiled.

"Hungry, no. Starving . . . yes! Thank you so much, Suzanne," he said with a grin. Royce opened his little care package and took a big bite.

"Amazing!" he yelled over the wind. "Did you make this?"

"Absolutely. Incredible what 'old maids' can do," she said with a laugh. "Now hang on, we're going to cruise through St. John's—our capital city—and it's a little tight between the buildings and houses."

Royce immediately saw what she was talking about. As the jeep started moving through the crowded streets of St. John's, he was quickly feeling claustrophobic.

People were everywhere. Fruit stands, markets, and pop-up shops seemed to be crowding every square inch of the downtown area. As they zipped through an alley, then turned quickly down an obscure little side street, Royce saw that Suzanne was now headed toward open green space, leaving the noisy, congested city behind.

"That's some serious driving! I don't think I've had a chauffeur drive me anywhere like that since I was in Casablanca. I'm still mentally recovering from that one, twenty-five years later, by the way." Royce laughed.

Suzanne laughed, too. But as she pulled up to a stop sign just outside the city, Royce's demeanor quickly changed. Looking to his left, he was stunned by what he saw.

"Suzanne . . . what is *that*? I mean, how did it get there?"

Suzanne looked and saw that Royce was pointing to a white banner, about four feet tall and eight feet wide, held up by a couple of sturdy wooden poles. On the banner was a picture of . . . Godfrey Tillman! Below it in large bold letters were the words: FAREWELL SIR GODFREY TILLMAN, YOU WILL BE MISSED BY ALL ANTIGUANS.

Suzanne paused, then said, "In my country, it's customary to honor people this way—especially those who have made a significant contribution to the lives of people on the island. Mr. Tillman was certainly one of those heroes."

Royce responded quickly, "But, 'Sir' Godfrey Tillman? I don't understand. . ."

Suzanne's expression became pensive. "Royce, as I said, there are a lot of things you need to learn about. Please be patient, and just know that Mr. Tillman made more of a difference in the world than you can imagine. Remember his words to you: 'Let everything unfold as it should.' "

How did she know Godfrey said those words to me? he wondered.

Royce took a deep breath, glanced once more at the banner, then calmly put on his sunglasses and nodded to Suzanne. "Let's go, my friend. It seems I have a lot to take in—and I'm ready to get started."

"Very good, Royce." Suzanne turned the jeep to the right, looked up at a sign pointing to Nelson's Dockyard ten miles away, then firmly pressed the accelerator.

"I remember Godfrey told me during our conversation that he lived near Nelson's Dockyard. I guess that's where we're heading?" asked Royce with an inquisitive look.

"Close," she responded neutrally. "Nelson's Dockyard is one of the beautiful ports that the British were so proud of during the eighteen hundreds. It's now a national park that people come from all over to see. However, Mr. Tillman lived in Shirley Heights, a few miles up the mountain from the port."

"Of course!" Royce replied. "Shirley Heights is one the most photographed points in the Caribbean. Looking out from the top of the mountain there, you can see not only Nelson's Dockyard, but half the island

and its beautiful cliffs, and crystal-clear ocean, if what I've read is correct."

"Yes," she replied with a smile. "It's true. Mr. Tillman's home is a stone's throw from there, but it was a well-kept secret. That's exactly how he wanted it."

Royce nodded. "I remember those words from him at Jekyll."

Suzanne nodded in turn, and after a few moments on the narrow, winding road, she smoothly veered off onto an unmarked dirt lane, densely lined with lush trees and wild, colorful plants—and more hibiscus.

"Hibiscus is the national flower here, in case you were wondering," she said with a broad grin.

"Yes, I noticed they're everywhere—and so many colors! The only thing I see more of is banana trees."

"Well, I've got a little more Antiguan trivia for you: bananas are actually called 'figs' here."

"Wait . . . what? Are you trying to tease an old country boy?" Royce laughed.

"Nope. True story," she retorted with a smile. "Now hold on, country boy—we're going deep into the rainforest, and these roads can get a little rough. Shirley Heights is just a few minutes away."

Suzanne wheeled into the tropical landscape, expertly navigating the dirt road with its large potholes. Occasionally, branches from the endless tunnel of trees would swipe at the jeep, causing Royce to duck.

"Fight those limbs off, Royce, we're almost there," she said with a grin.

At that moment, they exited the thick forest, and Suzanne abruptly stopped the vehicle. Royce looked in astonishment at what lay before him. He and Suzanne were now outside the gate of a large, beautiful Mediterranean-style home, surrounded by a variety of massive palm trees and several gardens full of multi-hued flowers. Not only were the grounds immaculately landscaped, but the house sat near the edge of a cliff, which only enhanced the magnificence of the entire scene.

Suzanne looked at Royce with a smile, then pulled slightly ahead. The gate opened slowly, and the vehicle edged forward a few more yards. Once the entrance was fully open, Suzanne pulled in and continued until the jeep reached the northern edge of the property. Then Royce stepped out while Suzanne sat quietly, waiting for his reaction.

Royce surveyed the view of the Caribbean Sea from east to west. "It's like nothing I've ever seen," he said in awe.

"Yes, it is incredible, isn't it? I never get tired of it here," she said with a sigh.

Royce looked over across the property and then down to his right, where he could see a part of the coastline, seemingly miles below where he was standing. "Is that Nelson's Dockyard down there?"

"Yes." Looking up from that landmark, she pointed across the property and added, "Also, if you look over to your right, Shirley Heights is just around the corner, through the rainforest. There's a path that almost no one knows about starting on the back corner of our property, which goes across the edge of the cliff and ends up over there. The view from that point is exactly as you described earlier. However," she said with a wink, "I think the view from Mr. Tillman's property is even better."

"I'm sure you're right," Royce said, still in a state of disbelief.

"I'll be right back." Suzanne pulled away to park the jeep in the garage about thirty yards back from where they stood.

Royce looked around in amazement. Behind him was a stunning Caribbean home, to the right was a tropical rainforest that looked like something out of a travel magazine, and below was the vast blue sea, its gentle waters lapping against picturesque rocky cliffs. Thinking back over his travels around the globe, Royce realized he had seen a lot of spectacular scenery, but this . . . this seemed indescribably different.

His thoughts were interrupted by Suzanne's approaching footsteps.

"I can understand why Godfrey chose this place for an 'escape'," Royce said with a smile. "It's paradise."

"It *is* beautiful. But I think Mr. Tillman was happy no matter where he was. This location was just where he needed to be for a time—for many reasons," she said with a hint of a smile.

"I understand." Royce nodded and smiled back.

Just then, a small animal akin to a skinny, short-legged squirrel came running past the two of them, visibly startling Royce.

"What the heck was that?" he said with a wide-eyed look.

Suzanne laughed with delight. "One of our mongoose friends! You'll find them all over Antigua—thanks to the British. They were the ones that originally brought the mongoose over, to get rid of snakes. It worked so well that we now have no snakes at all on the island."

"Well, there's another plus for this little slice of heaven. I hate snakes," Royce said with a frown.

Suzanne laughed. "I'll second that." Then, turning and starting to walk back toward the large home, she added with a tone of intrigue, "Royce, let's get your suitcase out of the jeep and head up into the house. There are some things I'd like you to see."

CHAPTER 3

After grabbing his luggage, Royce followed Suzanne up the stairs in the garage that led into the home. As she opened the door, she turned back to look at Royce, and with a sweeping gesture toward the interior, she said, "I hope you'll find it suitable for anything you might need during your stay."

Royce stepped inside and was immediately taken aback by the sheer grandeur of the abode. They now stood in an elegantly modern and spacious kitchen, beautifully adorned in island decor, and the floor was sparkling pure white marble. Walking into the room, Royce looked to the far end and saw a striking antique cherry kitchen table, clearly hand crafted, next to a large bay window. As he approached and looked outside, the view was the same as when standing overlooking the cliffs—simply spectacular. Ocean stretched out in shimmering blue as far as the eye could see. Again, he could look down and see Nelson's Dockyard in the distance.

"Spectacular," he managed to get out.

Suzanne nodded. "Come on, I think you'll like the den also."

She led him into the next room, fully constructed of beautiful teak, and Royce saw elegantly framed pictures of probably fifty different animals on the walls. Seeing Royce's astonishment, Suzanne commented, "He was quite the animal lover—not a hunter at all. Each of those photographs was taken by Mr. Tillman as he traveled the world."

"They're all . . . superb. Just like this whole place," responded Royce.

At that moment, Royce's gaze landed upon a picture sitting on a desk near a window with a soothing view of the rainforest. In the black-and-white photograph, six men stood side by side, apparently of varying ethnicities, although he surmised that several of them were Indian.

Suzanne cast a poignant look toward the picture. "Those were Mr. Gandhi's original leaders in the movement. The picture was taken in Panaji, and it turned out to be the last time that they were all together. Mr. Tillman is on the far left, and on the far right is Livingston, Maya's father."

Royce was spellbound. He immediately recalled Panaji as the meeting place in India where the men came up with the concept of the Four Daily Pillars of Wisdom. He inched closer to the picture until he almost felt face to face with each of the men. As he looked at them, he was overcome with a variety of emotions, inducing a strangely trancelike effect on him. Oddly enough, he felt a deep and visceral kinship of spirit with the men in the picture. It even seemed as if he *knew* them.

After what seemed like minutes, Suzanne finally spoke. "Royce, are you alright?"

Royce quickly pulled up and away from the photograph, feeling like a child who had been caught with a hand in the cookie jar. "I, um . . . I'm sorry, Suzanne. There's just something about the picture that I can't quite describe. The feeling I have when I look at each of those gentlemen is unlike anything I've ever experienced in looking at a photo."

"I'm sure that's true," Suzanne said, gazing at Royce with a surprisingly understanding look.

But as Royce turned and followed Suzanne into the next room—a study that Godfrey Tillman had apparently set aside for her—what he saw on her desk made her perplexing comment completely understandable. Even from a distance, Royce would recognize that book anywhere.

It was *The Six Principles of Sacred Power*.

CHAPTER 4

Royce looked at Suzanne in apparent shock.

However, before he could speak, Suzanne said in a quiet yet confident tone, "Yes, Royce, I know the Six Principles."

Royce felt as if he were standing there with his mouth open. "But . . . how? From Godfrey, I assume?"

"Let's go in the kitchen and have a cup of coffee. It's late, so I'll make some decaf. Give me just a few minutes," she said with a smile.

Royce nodded, then followed Suzanne back to the kitchen and sat down at the table while she began making a fresh pot of coffee. Glancing out at the breaking waves of the Caribbean Sea, he turned back toward Suzanne. "So, when did you learn the Principles?" he asked gently.

She turned the pot on, and the brewing softly began as she walked over and sat beside Royce. "Shortly before Mr. Tillman left for his trip around the world—about six months ago. He knew in his heart that the journey would be his last, and he wanted me to have his copy and his knowledge of *The Six Principles of Sacred Power*.

Since each of the book owners, as you know, is allowed to pass their copy along upon their death, he felt it was the right time."

"Incredible. But I have to say, when I met you, I immediately sensed you embodied the traits from the book."

"Thank you, Royce. The book changed my life, as you can well understand."

"I do, indeed," Royce said with a smile.

At that moment, Suzanne looked down and saw the ruby ring on Royce's finger. "Your ring . . . did Mr. Tillman give it to you?"

Royce realized that Suzanne was not yet aware of the Four Daily Pillars of Wisdom, since she had just recently become privy to the Six Principles. "Yes, it was a last request he had—for me to have the ring after our time together at Jekyll Island. I resisted at first, but it was futile." Royce smiled softly.

Tears rolled down Suzanne's cheeks as she envisioned Godfrey parting with the treasured ring. She managed an understanding smile. "Oh, yes, he was persuasive, to say the least. I know he would be proud that you wear it."

Royce nodded, then in a gentle tone, he asked, "So, may I ask how you met him?"

She dried her eyes, speaking slowly. "I suppose it was eighteen years ago. I had graduated from high school here in Antigua, but I couldn't afford to go beyond that, so I got a job cleaning houses. I did that for five years, barely making enough money to afford a small apartment in the poorest section of St. John's. It was horrible, actually . . . but I will say that those five years gave me a sense of strength that I probably couldn't have gotten any other way."

Royce leaned in, listening intently.

"Then one day, I received a phone call from Mr. Tillman. He said he was moving to Antigua, and somehow he had heard about me. He asked if I would be interested in applying for the job of keeping his home. So, I met with him, and I immediately sensed something special about this man—although at that time, I knew nothing about him or his relationship to *The Six Principles of Sacred Power*, of course. Well, he hired me on the spot, and he even gave me a room to live in! The longer I was here, the more I realized how special he really was. I became more than a housekeeper to him; he treated me like a beloved daughter. He took an interest in me, asking all about the skills I had. When I told him of some of those skills, he eventually allowed me to also become his personal assistant. As you can imagine, he kept an incredibly busy schedule, so there was much that needed to be done."

"So, you were responsible for the house—*and* for Mr. Tillman. That's quite a job!"

Suzanne laughed as she stood up to get the freshly made coffee. "You're right, I did get really good at being organized! Cream and sugar, Royce?"

"Just black, please," he replied with a smile.

Suzanne brought the full cups back to the table and continued, "Mr. Tillman, as you know, was an incredibly generous man. He did more for people on this island than I could ever explain. After the hurricane we had ten years ago, he helped rebuild homes and businesses all over Antigua. He also sponsored orphanages and schools. There was no end to his giving."

Royce nodded. "I can fully believe that. But Suzanne, was he *knighted*? I mean, the banner by the road in St. John's referred to him as 'Sir' Godfrey Tillman!"

She paused, looking pensively out the window for several seconds, then looked back at Royce. "That probably hurt him more than any other thing in his life—aside from losing his wife."

With a puzzled look, Royce added, "Godfrey told me at Jekyll Island about his wife leaving him, but he never mentioned being knighted. When you say it hurt him, what do you mean? What happened?"

"Did he tell you about the business he inherited from his father?" she asked.

"Yes, he told me it was a shipping business."

She smiled. "It wasn't just *any* shipping business. He grew the business into an empire. It was the best-known shipping business in the world."

"I had no idea," Royce said with a look of awe.

"That doesn't surprise me; he was the humblest of men. Well, the business was so successful that it eventually received contracts from the British government. The work Godfrey did was incredibly helpful to the Crown—so much so that he was knighted for his work. Hence, he became *Sir* Godfrey Tillman."

Royce's surprise was obvious as Suzanne continued. "Mr. Tillman did a great deal of humanitarian work with the Indian people, which the British monarchy despised. However, as I'm sure you're aware, the Brits never had any idea how *much* monetary help he was giving, or how involved he was in Mr. Gandhi's movement. But once the British government felt like they had enough information to connect him to the peaceful resistance, they brought treason charges against him. Those charges were eventually dropped, but part of the agreement was that he had to give up his knighthood. He was devastated."

Royce protested, "If they'd had any idea what kind of person he was, they would have never—"

"They didn't *care* what type of person he was," Suzanne interrupted him. "That was the irony of the whole thing. They were simply interested in money, politics, and preserving their hold on India—at all costs."

Royce nodded. "And I'm sure that gave him even more motivation to help the Indian people."

"Yes," she agreed. "Then, after the revolution, Mr. Tillman moved here and never looked back. He loved Antigua from the day he arrived."

"I can understand why," Royce concurred. "I've never seen any place like it!"

Suzanne smiled. "It's also why the banners on the side of the road read 'Sir Godfrey Tillman.' The people of Antigua believed in Godfrey—they loved and honored him—so in their minds, he deserved to keep his knighthood designation. To Antiguans, he was truly a knight in shining armor."

"Just wonderful!" said Royce. "He made an impact wherever he went, didn't he?"

"Yes, he did. But now we find ourselves in the painful and challenging position of carrying on without him, which we must do. Mr. Tillman's body will arrive here tomorrow, and I've followed his requests to the letter. He asked to be cremated upon arrival—which I have arranged—and then to have his ashes cast over the Caribbean Sea, from the back part of this property. The only people he wanted to witness this were me, you, and a young priest from the local Anglican church."

Although he was grateful for the gesture, a feeling of deep sadness came over Royce as the reality of Godfrey's death once again sank in. "I'm honored," he humbly declared.

"As am I," affirmed Suzanne. "Mr. Tillman was known all over the globe, but he was also a very private person, so his wanting to have just a few people at his service doesn't surprise me. But I assure you, if he had requested the service to be open to the world, Antigua couldn't hold the number of people who would come to pay their respects and show their gratitude."

Royce nodded. "He changed so many lives. . ."

As Suzanne nodded in agreement, Royce circled back to his earlier question. "Suzanne, can you tell me more about why I am here? How am I able to help fulfill Godfrey's request? Do you know?"

Suzanne's look became serious. "Yes, I do know why Mr. Tillman wanted you to be here."

Royce cocked his head and raised an eyebrow.

She continued, "You may assume that all copies of *The Six Principles of Sacred Power* have been passed on to the next generation of book owners."

"Right," he agreed.

"Well, that's not quite true." Suzanne paused and then slowly added, "Let me explain."

Royce braced himself as Suzanne took a deep breath and began telling an extraordinary story. . .

CHAPTER 5

Royce couldn't imagine what Suzanne was about to share, but his blank look encouraged her to continue.

"Almost every book *is* accounted for. They are in the hands of each of the people Sir Godfrey visited on his way to Jekyll Island . . . except for one copy."

Royce's head was spinning as he tried to think which copy she could possibly be referring to. "Which one?" he finally asked with urgency.

Suzanne paused. "Mr. Gandhi's personal copy."

"What?" Royce blurted out, visibly shocked.

"Mr. Gandhi knew that his personal tome of *The Six Principles of Sacred Power* would be a significant historical relic. Thus, he did not hand it down to anyone. Instead, he directed in his will that the book be passed on to Livingston for safekeeping, and then upon Livingston's passing, to Godfrey Tillman to safely protect the book."

"This is incredible," said Royce.

"I know," Suzanne replied. "Mr. Tillman eventually shared with me that the book had been hidden by Livingston in Sri Lanka. Ironically, it seems it was hidden in the same shop where the books were originally published clandestinely by Mr. Gandhi's law school friend. I don't know exactly where the manuscript was hidden in the shop, but it was so carefully tucked away that Godfrey had a hard time finding it after Livingston's death—even with explicit instructions."

Royce clearly was still trying to take in everything he was hearing. "So, Mr. Gandhi knew the book would be *that* sought after, that it should be hidden with such precision?"

"Yes. Plus, being as it was the personal copy of Mahatma Gandhi, the book would likely be one of the most valued antiquities on the planet. I have heard it estimated that it would fetch over a hundred million US dollars if it were somehow brought to market. Mr. Gandhi also wisely assumed it might eventually be sought out by the wrong people—even though the existence of all the books was supposedly a carefully guarded secret. Therefore, he went to great lengths to protect the location of the book, as did Livingston, and now Sir Godfrey has done the same thing. Actually, Godfrey may have gone to even greater lengths to conceal and protect it than Livingston or Mr. Gandhi himself did."

"And I assume you know where Godfrey hid the book?" Royce asked matter-of-factly.

She shook her head solemnly. "No, Royce, I don't."

"What? Well, then, who does?"

"No one that I am aware of."

Royce stared in disbelief. "*No* one? Then how is the book ever going to be located?"

Suzanne smiled softly. "You are going to find it."

"Now, wait a minute!" said Royce, flabbergasted. "*I* am going to find it . . . ?"

"That's right. It's what Mr. Tillman wanted. With the confidence Maya had in you, Sir Godfrey believed without question that you were the right person to safely preserve this magnificent treasure for the next generation. However, he knew he had to be cryptic with his instructions on finding where he has hidden the book—although I do know for a fact that it is in Antigua."

Royce thoughtfully rubbed his chin. "Well, I guess knowing it's on the island somewhere does narrow it down a bit, since Antigua is only one hundred and seventy square miles," he said with a laugh. "But if you're serious—and I'm still not sure about that—where would I even start looking? I mean, talk about finding a needle in a haystack!"

Suzanne's tone became firm. "Royce, forgive me, but I must say that those are words of doubt. You have gifts now that few other people have. You have mastered abilities that most people never even realize are available to them. Your faith can move mountains! All the traits you uncovered in Maya's teachings from *The Six Principles of Sacred Power* are at your disposal now, and I must believe that the words Mr. Tillman shared with you at Jekyll Island surely back that up. Royce, who in the world could be more prepared for this journey than you?"

Royce sat quietly, absorbing Suzanne's words. He knew in his heart that she was right. He *was* prepared—whether he admitted it or not. If Maya and Godfrey had taught him anything, it was that he had the potential to do things most people would think were utterly impossible.

Royce smiled gently. "You're pretty convincing, you know that?"

Suzanne grinned. "I learned from the best."

Royce shook his head and smiled even wider. "Ok, I'll do it! But, Suzanne, where in the world do I begin . . . ?"

Suzanne paused, then quietly said, "Royce, it's getting late, and I know this is a lot to take in. We'll discuss it more tomorrow."

Royce started to speak, but Suzanne gently interrupted him. "Don't ask questions, for it will all become clear to you—every step of the way. Just continue to trust. Now more than ever. . ."

Looking at him with calmness and compassion, she stood up and quietly excused herself for the night. As Royce stood up to do the same, he suddenly had an eerie recollection that the words she had just spoken were the final words that Sir Godfrey Tillman had shared with him at Jekyll Island.

CHAPTER 6

After a night of much-needed sleep, Royce awoke the next morning with mixed emotions. He was beyond excited for the journey he was about to embark on, but he was also feeling deeply sad, knowing that Godfrey's funeral service was imminent. He knew it would be a difficult event for him, regardless of how much Mr. Tillman had wanted it to be a time of celebration.

Getting out of bed, he walked over to the window of the guest room, took in the gorgeous ocean view, and then, as Godfrey had instructed him at Jekyll, he began reciting the Four Daily Pillars of Wisdom:

- *Today, I will choose to respond in peace, no matter what challenges occur in my life.*
- *Today, I will choose to look for and honor the good in every person I meet, realizing each of us is doing the best we possibly can.*
- *Today, I will choose to greet each situation with courage, knowing that everything I want and need lies in overcoming my fears.*
- *Today, I will choose to trust that everything that happens in my life is designed to make me a stronger, wiser, more compassionate person.*

It was fascinating to Royce how those words always brought an immediate feeling of peace. It affirmed to him that the founding group of leaders had known exactly what they were doing years ago in Panaji, when they formulated these specific four pillars to capture and evoke the spirit of *The Six Principles of Sacred Power*.

Stepping away from the window, Royce turned and walked downstairs. As he reached the bottom of the staircase, he looked around in admiration at the beautiful island home, then realized he was still feeling a bit out of place. It was, after all, Godfrey's home, and although Suzanne made him feel like an extremely welcome guest, he still was just a visitor here.

Reaching the kitchen, he was immediately absorbed in the tantalizing aroma of bacon cooking, and it brought back memories of his mother's delectable Southern breakfasts when he was growing up on the Georgia coast. Stepping into the room, he saw Suzanne at the stove in a green apron, singing softly while she cooked. Hearing Royce's footsteps, she turned and said with a smile, "Good morning, sleepyhead! It's almost nine thirty. I was wondering when you would wake up."

Royce yawned and managed a grin. "I feel like I got hit by a train last night! I guess travel really takes it out of you sometimes. What time is the service?"

"It's at noon. But it's only a five-minute walk through the woods to that part of Shirley Heights," she added. "We have plenty of time. I talked to the priest briefly this morning, and he said the service would be quite simple, but there are a couple of things Mr. Tillman had specifically asked to be done."

Royce cocked his head to the side.

Suzanne shrugged. "I don't really know what he was referring to, but I guess we'll find out soon."

"Hmmm . . . guess so," agreed Royce.

"Here's a cup of coffee." Suzanne handed him a mug of the dark brew. "Have a seat at the table, and I'll bring your breakfast over in a few minutes."

"Thank you," Royce said with a nod and a smile. He walked over to the kitchen table and sat down, once again marveling at the view. "My gosh, the sky and the water . . . they're just breathtaking this morning!"

Suzanne laughed. "Almost every morning is like this! Antigua weather is virtually the same year-round."

"Wonderful! I could get used to this. . ."

At that moment, he caught sight of a small land mass in the distance with a lighthouse on it. "What's that island?" he asked.

Suzanne walked over from her cooking and looked where Royce was pointing. "Ah, that's Redonda Island. At one point, it was a flourishing little outpost for the British. Not much left there now. In fact, the only person remaining is a lighthouse keeper, who I understand has been on the job for over fifty years!"

"Now, that's some serious dedication!" Royce said with a smile.

"For sure." Moving over to the stove, Suzanne admired the breakfast she had prepared and announced, "Ok, Royce, I think it's ready! I'll serve you."

Royce smiled broadly. "I could get used to this, too."

"Don't get *too* used to it," Suzanne playfully shot back, and the two laughed.

Suzanne placed the dishes of food on the table and sat down with Royce. There was a large bowl of local mangos, papayas, black pineapple, and bananas, and an enticing basket of homemade bread, along with sizzling bacon and eggs.

"This looks delicious, Suzanne!" Royce commented appreciatively.

Suzanne smiled. "It's my pleasure. I hope you enjoy it."

As they began eating, Royce asked, "How do you feel your time spent with Mr. Tillman influenced you?"

"Oh, it influenced me on every level you can think of. I mean, when he met me, I was just a poor maid with very little knowledge of the 'real world.' Sir Godfrey not only guided me from a personal standpoint, but he also showed me the power each of us has from a spiritual perspective. I observed it in the way he lived his everyday life—especially in how he interacted with other people. He had such a genuine spirit of compassion and empathy for them."

"Yes, I realized that very quickly when I met him at Jekyll."

Suzanne nodded. "Of course, later, when he shared *The Six Principles of Sacred Power* with me, I understood even more. He truly was destined to meet Livingston and Mr. Gandhi—and to be privy to the book."

"Did you ever meet Livingston—or Maya?" Royce asked.

"No, Livingston had passed before my time with Mr. Tillman, and to my knowledge, Maya has never been to the island. However, I heard so much about them both that I feel like I've known them."

"I understand," said Royce. "Plus, surely anyone who has direct contact with *The Six Principles of Sacred Power* has a unique connection with others who have also been exposed to it."

Suzanne smiled. "I suppose you're right. And those similar traits in each of us likely stem from the commonalities Mr. Gandhi found in the teachings of the great spiritual masters, wouldn't you say?"

"Undoubtedly," replied Royce.

Suzanne paused, then hesitantly asked, "Tell me, what is Maya like?"

Royce thought for a few seconds. "I guess you could say she's the type of person we all want to be like. She embodies all the traits of the Six Principles in a way that I feel must be unique."

Suzanne nodded. "So, you got to spend time with her in her gardens—seven days, if I heard correctly. I just can't imagine what it would be like to be able to spend that amount of time with a woman like her."

Royce agreed. "It was a week that changed me forever. Her kindness, compassion, and inner strength were inspiring. As a teacher, she had a gift for guiding people in the right direction, without forcing them to an outcome. I suppose the only way I can repay her for what she did for me is to share her type of spirit and attitude wherever I go, with whomever I meet—at least, to the best of my ability."

Suzanne smiled, then said with a sigh, "Maybe someday I can meet her, too. . ."

Royce smiled in return and offered, "I truly hope so, Suzanne. I imagine you two would have a lot in common."

Just then, Suzanne glanced at her watch. "Oh my, we've got to get going, Royce! Time is getting away from us."

As they each pushed away from the table, Royce said to Suzanne, "I'll help with the dishes; it's the least I can do after a meal like that!"

Suzanne seemed to blush as she said with a smile, "Thank you, Royce, but you go and do what you need to do. I'll handle this. It's not my first rodeo, as you say in America."

Royce grinned. "I'll meet you back downstairs in about an hour, and we'll walk over together."

"Deal," she replied, grinning back at him, and Royce headed hurriedly up the stairs.

It was a brisk walk from the house through the rainforest to the site of the service, but along the way, Royce couldn't help but marvel at the surrounding beauty. The lushness, the vibrant colors, and the wide variety of tropical plants and trees were breathtakingly different from anything Royce had ever experienced. When the two arrived at the funeral site—a peaceful grassy knoll overlooking the sea—the priest, a blonde, fit-looking young man with a British accent, greeted them with an outstretched hand. "I'm Andrew," he said with a smile. "You must be Suzanne and Royce."

The two nodded solemnly.

"I want to offer my sincere condolences. Sir Godfrey not only meant a great deal to me—and to our church—but the whole island has already felt the loss."

"Yes, it was quite a shock. But he left so much goodness wherever he went. I am grateful to have known him," Suzanne replied softly.

The minister smiled in agreement, and the three of them engaged in some small talk and reminiscing.

After a few moments, the priest walked over to a little table and picked up a light green ceramic urn, then approached the edge of the cliff. He looked back at Royce and Suzanne, motioning for them to join him.

Once they all stood assembled atop the cliff, Andrew spoke some eloquent, heartfelt words of praise for Godfrey. Every sentiment about Godfrey's compassion, courage, and wisdom had Royce and Suzanne nodding and smiling in agreement. When he had finished, Andrew slowly lifted the urn toward the sky. Then in one quick yet gentle movement, he flung the ashes over the cliff and out toward the vast Caribbean Sea below.

Royce stood pensive and motionless for a few seconds, then in a barely audible voice, he uttered, "A citizen of the world now, indeed. How fortunate I am to have known this spiritual giant."

Suzanne reached over and softly squeezed Royce's hand. Then, with tears in her eyes, she looked out to the ocean and said in a hushed tone, "Goodbye, my mentor and friend. Godspeed on your journey."

A moment of silence followed, after which the young priest looked at Royce and Suzanne, then offered with a caring smile, "This concludes our simple service, as Sir Godfrey requested. Let us go in peace and live our lives in a way that would make him proud."

Royce and Suzanne nodded, thanked Andrew, and took turns shaking his hand in gratitude.

As the pair walked away, Royce heard the voice of the priest calling after him, "Mr. Holloway, there *is* one more thing. . ."

Turning back, Royce saw the young man reaching out with an envelope in hand. "Sir Godfrey asked me to give this to you."

As Royce accepted the envelope, his puzzled look didn't go unnoticed by Andrew, yet the priest simply smiled, turned, and quietly walked away.

Royce looked at Suzanne, whose neutral countenance gave nothing away. He opened the small white envelope and scanned the words.

After a few seconds, he began reading aloud with a confused expression.

> *Dear Royce,*
>
> *At this point, I am sure I owe you a "thank you" for coming to my little island and attending this service. I am grateful, and it affirms once again that Maya's words of exceeding approval of you were quite accurate.*
>
> *I am honored that you have taken on this quest, which Suzanne has shared with you. Of course, to ensure the site of Mr. Gandhi's book remains a secret, my "map" for its location had to be extremely obscure. Only one person in the world knows where the book resides, and to help you find that person, you'll meet some extraordinary friends of mine who will point you in the right direction.*
>
> *Odd as it may sound now, I suggest you savor this journey to retrieve the sacred book. What you'll learn along the way to your ultimate destination will prove valuable to you later—and to many others.*
>
> *Now, Royce, the first person you must meet is Dianne LeCraw. You will find her at 160 East Bay's Edge in St. John's.*
>
> *Until we meet again. . .*
>
> *Godfrey*

Folding the letter back up, Royce glanced reflectively at Suzanne, then the two of them walked the short distance back to the house in silence.

Stepping inside the home, Suzanne looked at Royce, saying evenly, "Seems as if you have an expedition ahead of you."

"I suppose you're right," Royce casually replied. "I think I'll go upstairs and pack some things in case I'm gone for a few days; sounds like that's a distinct possibility. Mind if I leave a suitcase here?"

"Of course not," Suzanne replied with a smile. "Anything I can do to help, just let me know—although I'm not sure how much help I would really be. I was never good at treasure hunts as a kid."

Royce smiled back at her. As he walked up the stairs to gather his items for the journey, he began wondering what adventure lay ahead for him *this time*. . .

CHAPTER 7

Suzanne had been kind enough to proactively call a cab for Royce, and in just a few moments, the small black car arrived, as if it had been nearby waiting for her request. After a quick goodbye to Suzanne, Royce hopped in the waiting vehicle, gave the driver the address of the destination, and headed off the property on his ride back into St. John's.

The Antiguan cab driver was a good-looking young man who appeared to be in his late twenties, with dreadlocked hair and a slim build. Although he had a pleasant countenance, he wasn't too talkative, but that suited Royce just fine. Royce's mind was full of curious thoughts about the impending visit with Dianne LeCraw. He couldn't imagine what she would be like—or what she would possibly have to share with him.

When they arrived at his destination, Royce saw that the driver had pulled up in front of a florist's shop, and he gave the man a puzzled look. "Are you sure we're in the right place?"

The cabbie chuckled and replied with a thick Antiguan accent, "This is it, my friend: 160 East Bay's Edge. Want to go somewhere else?"

"No," Royce replied neutrally. "This will be fine." He stepped out of the vehicle, walked around to the driver's open window, and gave the young man twenty American dollars. "Keep the change," he offered.

The cabbie smiled and nodded, then slowly pulled away, the car blending into the noisy city traffic.

Royce stood alone in front of the small brown storefront, staring up at the FLORIST sign, wondering if he really *was* in the right place. Nevertheless, he opened the front door and stepped inside. A small bell on the door tinkled cheerfully, signaling the entrance of a visitor in the quaint little shop. As soon as he entered, he immediately felt relaxed and comfortable. Looking around the surprisingly spacious store, he noticed the wide variety of magnificent plants and flowers, the perfectly organized shelves of gardening accessories, the colorful Caribbean murals on the walls, and a luscious floral smell wafting through the place.

A petite young woman with short brown hair and wire-rimmed glasses—looking more like a librarian than a florist—emerged from the back. She flashed a broad smile as she wiped her hands on her apron, calling out gleefully, "Afternoon!" in a clearly American accent.

Happy to hear a familiar voice, he replied, "Good afternoon to you, too! I'm looking for Dianne LeCraw."

"Look no further," she replied with a grin.

Royce smiled. "Well, that was easy enough. A friend of mine sent me to see you, and I wasn't exactly sure who I'd be meeting. I'm Royce Holloway."

The woman paused. "How nice. Who is your friend?" she asked with an inquisitive expression.

"Godfrey Tillman," Royce replied with a smile.

With wide eyes and a big grin, Dianne spontaneously reached out and hugged the unsuspecting Royce. "Mr. Holloway! I'm so happy to meet you!"

Royce smiled and sheepishly responded, "Wow, I wish I had that kind of effect on every woman I met!"

She laughed. "Well, I didn't know whom Sir Godfrey was sending, but I've been waiting for that person. What a pleasure to meet you!"

Royce looked at her with a countenance that showed he clearly didn't understand. "How did you know Mr. Tillman?"

She smiled, walked over to the door, and swiftly changed the shop sign to read CLOSED to potential customers, then turned back and led him to a small table. "I don't often close the shop at this time of day, but as it turns out, I sent my staff home to enjoy an unexpected paid day off, so I'm here working in their place. Please, sit down," she happily said. "I'd be honored to share how my connection with Sir Godfrey came about."

Royce smiled as he reflected on the business owner's generous gesture of a day off for her employees. "I love that you did that for your staff, Dianne—what a great idea!"

"Well, they deserve it, and more, so it's my pleasure." She beamed.

Royce sat down in a small wooden chair at the table, then leaned back and began listening as the young woman started her story.

"Let's see . . . where should I start? How about at the beginning?" she said with a grin. "I was born in Cleveland."

Royce gave a shiver. "I hope this story gets warmer," he said with a laugh. "I'm from Atlanta, and *that's* cold enough for me in the winter, much less Ohio!"

She laughed also. "Believe me, I couldn't wait to go south! From the time I was in my teens, I dreamed of being in a place with warm weather. The winters were so brutal in Cleveland; I just knew I wanted to get away as quickly as I could."

Royce nodded and smiled.

"When I graduated from college, I thought I was ready to conquer the world! I got a business degree, and my parents gave me a little money, so I decided I would take off and start a business down here—live the 'easy island life,' you know?"

"So far, so good," Royce quipped with a grin.

"Right. The problem was that I didn't know as much about business as I thought I did. Sure, I knew flowers, and I had worked in flower shops and nurseries, but. . ."

"Big difference between working for a business and *owning* a business, huh?" interjected Royce.

"Oh, you said it! I didn't understand the financial side, or the customer service side, or the marketing side, like I thought college had prepared me for. I thought my passion for flowers and a basic degree would be enough. I tell folks it's like someone saying, 'I love good food; I think I'll open a restaurant. Dianne laughed and rolled her eyes. "Well, at that time, I had this same little florist's shop that you're sitting in now, and my bills started piling up. I panicked. I started losing employees, and I was basically about to lose my whole store . . . plus, I was about to lose my mind.

"One day, when my spirits were at their lowest and I was ready to give up and move back home, Mr. Tillman walked in. Turns out he was buying some flowers for Ms. Dismont's birthday, and after he picked out his flowers and walked up to the counter, he saw me standing there—and I must've looked like a hot mess."

Royce leaned forward, listening with deep interest as she continued.

"He smiled at me, and somehow he knew immediately what was wrong. I still remember his words, and that wonderful British accent: 'Young lady, I think you could use some help.' For whatever reason—maybe I was simply desperate—I broke down and cried and told him that was exactly what I needed: *help*.

"Well, he sat down with me—at this very table—and I poured my heart out and told him the whole story of my dream to come here and open this shop, and how difficult times had gotten."

"And then . . . ?" Royce said with an apprehensive tone.

Dianne smiled, pulling her shoulders back with pride. "And then, Sir Godfrey Tillman gave me a plan. He said he would come by every day and teach me business, until things got back on track. He said he believed in me! Not only that, but he also lent me ten thousand dollars to invest in my fledgling little company!"

"Amazing!" Royce said with admiration. "One thing I saw in Godfrey was this deep desire to make a difference in peoples' lives, plus he had a unique intuition for knowing just what they needed."

"Exactly," she agreed with a broad smile. "He taught me so many things that I wasn't even aware I needed to know. I learned how to empower my team, which in turn led to them inspiring my customers. I learned how to systematize, organize, and prioritize my projects, so that I felt like I was in control of the business, rather than the business being in control of *me*. I think the experts call it learning to work *on* the business, rather than *in* the business every day."

"What was the result?" Royce asked eagerly.

Dianne beamed. "The result? Well, my business began to prosper in so many ways! My wonderful staff became proud of where they were working. With Mr. Tillman's guidance, they became proficient in all aspects of the enterprise. Today, because of that, many of them even own their own businesses! People come from across St. John's just to see my amazing little store and to feel the great energy here. Before Sir Godfrey, I felt as if I had the Sword of Damocles hanging over me every day, with all that horrible pressure. After his help, I felt I had a shop that was now an enjoyable asset, rather than a personally draining liability. I began loving being a business owner—like I had dreamed of being."

Royce leaned back and smiled. "What an incredible story! Hearing what Godfrey did for you affirms everything I believed about him—even though I knew him only a short while."

"Wonderful. And to me, you know what the greatest thing about it was?" she asked with a smile.

"What's that?"

"Everything Sir Godfrey did for me, he did in a way that made me feel valued, appreciated, and respected. It wasn't like I was some pity project that he was taking on. I realized that what he was doing for my business was also helping me become a better person, and by helping me become the best that I could be, he was grooming me to do the same for others when I had the opportunity. Even though he was incredibly busy with so many other projects, I seemed to be all that mattered to him at that time—like he had an unwavering dedication to making sure I succeeded . . . which, gratefully, I did. I now have eight stores across the island, and each of them employ dedicated, talented local people who have the same types of dreams I did when I first entered the business all those years ago. Plus, every store you walk into feels, smells, and looks the same; each one is the type of place that people love to shop in."

Royce looked at Dianne in admiration. "You must be very proud."

"Well, yes," she said. "But there's no time for self-congratulations; there's always plenty of work to be done." She looked at her watch. "Oh my. . . Speaking of work to be done, I'd better get back to it. I feel like I've talked your ear off, but there's one more thing. . ."

Royce watched curiously as she reached into her purse that was sitting off to the side of the table. She then pulled out a small envelope and handed it to him. "I believe this is for you," she happily offered.

Surprised, Royce reached out and accepted the envelope, then started to open it. At that point, Dianne stood up and said, "I'll let you have a little privacy. See you in a few minutes!"

Royce opened the envelope carefully, with some trepidation. As he pulled out the note inside, he began reading, and he could almost hear Godfrey's voice in the words:

Dear Royce,

Well done, my good man!

If you are reading this, you were able to meet Dianne LeCraw—and what a splendid woman she is! She has changed many lives, and my time with her was unforgettable. She was fiercely determined to succeed, and yet in addition to that fierceness, she had a kind, compassionate heart. I trust your time with her was worth the effort, and I have no doubt your paths will cross in the future.

Now, it is time to move on to the next person on your journey. You will find a gentleman named Gifford Witherspoon at a small inn called Somerset Point, just outside of St. John's. I recommend you spend a night at the inn—it is very special—and then look for Gifford in the morning.

Carry on,

Godfrey

Royce slowly folded the note and put it back in the envelope. Standing up, he walked to the front of the store and found Dianne standing at the counter.

Smiling, she politely said, "I trust the letter provided you with what you needed, Royce."

"I think it did," he said with a smile. "Now I'll need to be on my way, I suppose, but it was an honor to meet you, Dianne. In just this short period of time together, I can tell we have a lot in common."

"Well," she said, "any friend of Sir Godfrey's is a friend of mine. It's as if he imparted a little piece of his loving spirit to others wherever he went."

"I believe it," Royce replied with a smile. "Thank you again, Dianne."

Dianne nodded and smiled. "My pleasure, Royce."

With that, Royce opened the door and walked out to the sidewalk to hail a cab to take him to his next stop. But to his surprise, the same cab driver from earlier was parked right in front of him, apparently waiting for Royce.

The cabbie rolled down his window and laughed. "What a coincidence, wouldn't you say? Shall I take you to Somerset Point, my friend?"

Royce stood and stared in disbelief. "Wait . . . how did you—"

The driver put up his hand as if to stop him, and with a big grin, he said, "I'll take that as a yes, then. Jump in."

"Ok, Somerset Point it is!" Royce smiled and shook his head. Throwing his bag into the back seat, he plopped down next to it and closed the door.

Turning on some reggae, the young, lanky driver slowly eased the car out into the St. John's traffic, guiding the vehicle toward their destination, which he said was about ten miles outside St. John's.

"What's your name?" Royce asked inquisitively.

"Julian. And yours?"

"I'm Royce. Royce Holloway."

"Royce Holloway—the author? No way! I've read all your books!" the driver said with a huge smile. "Let's see. . . 'Nothing's a big deal unless I choose to make it a big deal.' That's your quote, right?"

"Yup," replied Royce with a chuckle, amazed by this serendipity. "You got it!"

The driver turned back to Royce and pointed to a small piece of paper taped to the dashboard. It was the exact same quote he had just shared with Royce. "I keep it in front of me, so I'm reminded of that truth when things get tough," the young driver added.

"Glad to hear it," Royce replied with a smile. "It's a good one for me to remember, too."

Julian nodded as he turned left onto an old dirt road, then made a quick right into some dense forest. After several miles, a small, tropical-looking structure with a thatched roof came into sight. The cabbie happily announced, "Here we are, Mr. Holloway: Somerset Point Inn. They say this is one of the most peaceful places in all of Antigua."

Royce tipped the driver, opened the door, then turned and replied, "Peacefulness—I could use that!" Then he added, "Want to pick me up tomorrow?"

"Sure," Julian said with a smile. "I'll be here."

Closing the door, Royce then stuck his head back through the open window and countered, "But . . . I don't even know what time yet."

Shrugging, the young man grinned. "Doesn't matter. I'll be here then."

With that, he pulled away through the jungle and left Royce standing in front of the small hotel, shaking his head again with a smile. A thought popped into his head: *Just allow it to unfold. Divine timing is always perfect.*

Taking a deep breath, Royce headed inside to see what—or who—might be waiting for him at the Somerset Point Inn.

CHAPTER 8

Royce walked through the lobby and up to the front desk, where he was greeted by a freckle-faced young man wearing glasses and sporting a stylish haircut. He appeared to be about twenty-five years old.

"Can I help you?" he quickly offered with a welcoming smile.

"Hi, I just need a room for the night."

"Great," replied the attendant, sliding a registration form across the desk. "Just fill this out for me."

As Royce completed the form, the clerk wrinkled his brow, looked down, and began thumbing through a small box of papers. Finding the document he sought, he pulled it out of the box, looked up at Royce, and said with a look of satisfaction, "I've got the perfect room for you: 53B. Best view at the inn."

Royce handed the completed registration form to the young man, gave him a high five, and took the key offered him. "Thanks, that sounds perfect. Just point me in the right direction."

The clerk led Royce back to the front door and stepped outside, pointing to the far end of the hotel.

"Go about fifty yards down that way, and then walk up the stairs to the second floor. Your room is on the end, overlooking the lagoon. You're just in time for sunset, if you hurry."

Royce thanked the young man, and as they each began to go their own ways, Royce suddenly stopped and turned. "By the way, do you happen to know Gifford Witherspoon?"

The clerk looked upward, as if he was trying to find the name somewhere in his brain. "Hmmm . . . I don't think so. Sorry."

Royce gave a puzzled look to the young man, but then thanked him and headed down the sidewalk to his room for the evening.

Once he reached 53B, Royce entered the room and was greeted with a big bowl of delectable tropical fruits, and another bowl full of nuts. He threw his travel bag on the bed, then opened the small refrigerator, where he saw a variety of cheeses and a small bottle of white wine.

"Well, I think I just figured out what to do for dinner," he said with a chuckle.

Stepping out onto the balcony, like the clerk had said, Royce saw the magnificent Caribbean sun starting to melt into the island horizon. Hurrying back inside, he opened the bottle of wine, poured a small serving in a plastic cup, grabbed the nuts, cheese, and a mango, and took it all out to the little porch. Placing his newfound goodies on a small table, he sat in a wicker lounge chair, picked up the wine, and held it out toward the setting sun. "Not bad," he said with a smile. "Not bad at all."

Then Royce's countenance became pensive as he added in a melancholy tone, "A toast to you, Sir Godfrey. May I continue to meet the people you'd like me to meet on this journey, and may I end up exactly where you'd like me to end up."

Just then, a slight breeze blew across the balcony, and as Royce felt the coolness on his face, it reminded him to savor the moment. He inhaled a deep, slow breath, closed his eyes, then relaxed back into his chair to listen to the peaceful sounds of the tropical twilight.

A couple of hours passed quickly, and after emptying the small bottle of wine, Royce decided to turn in for the evening. Hearing the crickets chirping and the waves breaking in the distance, he knew he would have no trouble getting a good night's rest. He stepped inside, brushed his teeth, washed his face, then fell sound asleep on the large, soft bed.

CHAPTER 9

Royce awoke to the waves crashing outside his room and the bright Caribbean sun beating in on him through the sliding glass door. Getting up, he sleepily walked over and peered out at the coastline, taking note of the many people already gathered there.

Man, they hit the beach early around here, he thought. *Wonder what time it is. . .* Glancing over at the clock on the nightstand, Royce's jaw dropped. Eleven o'clock!

"Well, I guess I was even more tired than I thought," he mused as he shook his head.

Jumping in the shower to wake up, Royce thought about the coming day. *I don't know where I'm going, when I'm supposed to get there, or how I'm supposed to find the person I need to meet next,* he thought. *Other than that, it seems like my day is perfectly planned out!* He laughed to himself.

After a few minutes, Royce emerged from the shower feeling refreshed. He put on a pair of khaki shorts and a T-shirt, ran a comb through his salt-and-pepper hair, and headed downstairs to the lobby to see if he could find a recommendation for an early lunch.

The same young clerk from the previous evening greeted Royce with a lively hello, and he suggested that the outdoor café near the pool might be a good choice for lunch. "They fix a tasty Creole chicken with peas," he offered with a smile.

"Sounds like a winner to me!" Royce responded enthusiastically.

The young clerk pointed to a side door. "Out that door and to the right. Shouldn't be busy now."

Royce nodded, smiled, and headed down the hall to the exit.

As he stepped outside, Royce noticed that the Antiguan sun was already heating things up. Walking over to the café, he saw a sign that read SEAT YOURSELF, so he plopped down in a cushioned wooden chair and picked up the menu lying on the glass tabletop. As he did, a young waitress with a gentle island dialect walked up and placed a large glass of orange juice in front of him.

"Fresh-squeezed today, sir," she proudly noted. "It's complimentary for our guests."

Royce took a sip and smiled. "Wow, that's some fresh juice, if I've ever had any! By the way, I hear y'all make some mighty good Creole chicken and peas. Got any on the menu today?"

"You better believe it! I'll bring some right out," she replied cheerfully, then turned and walked toward the kitchen to place Royce's order.

Just then, glancing to his left, he saw that a window washer had arrived and was beginning to set up by a large pane of glass across from the door Royce had just exited. The man appeared to be in his seventies, yet his nimble movements were that of a much younger man. Placing a pail of water beside himself, he gently and precisely began washing the window. Royce was enthralled as he watched the window washer work with the effortless grace of a tai chi master.

After a few minutes, the man put down his squeegee, picked up the pail, and began walking toward a spigot near Royce. As he passed, he smiled and said aloud, "Guess I underestimated my water needs for today! Hate it when that happens."

Royce nodded and smiled back, then noticed the words embroidered on his light brown baseball cap: GIFF'S WINDOW SERVICE.

Royce hesitated, then impulsively blurted out, "Excuse me, sir, are you Gifford?"

As if the man had expected the question, he paused and slowly pushed up the bill of his cap, and a broad grin came across his face. Royce noted that his Caribbean accent sounded slightly different from the other islanders as he replied, "That I am, my friend. Gifford Witherspoon's the name. You can call me Giff."

Royce smiled, stood, and extended his hand. "My name is Royce Holloway, and I think we have a mutual friend, Godfrey Tillman. Could you possibly sit and have lunch with me?"

The older man eased into an even broader smile. "Godfrey Tillman, huh? Well, it's just about lunchtime, and I have a feeling you and I may have some things to talk about. Plus, I've always wanted to try the Creole chicken here."

Royce laughed heartily. "With the reputation the Creole chicken has at this place, I'm surprised there's any poultry left on the island!"

Gifford grinned and sat down.

Seeing this, the waitress stopped back by the table, and Royce said, "My friend will have the same order as me, please. Put it on my tab."

She smiled, wrote down the request on a small pad, and headed back toward the kitchen.

"Well, I'm really not even sure where to begin," Royce admitted. "How did you know Mr. Tillman?"

The older man leaned back in his chair, crossed his arms, and seemed to be gathering his thoughts. "Sir Godfrey Tillman. Well . . . he changed my life," he slowly and thoughtfully began.

Giff immediately saw that he had Royce's attention, so he continued, "My wife and I lived in Jamaica with our two young boys. I was working long hours, trying to get us by, but times were hard on the island, and I could barely make a living."

Royce nodded with keen interest.

"At first, we thought we could just hang in there until things got better, but things *didn't* get better. I was washing windows for a company, and the pay was terrible, plus I had no opportunity for growth there. One day, my wife decided she'd had enough. She . . . gave up and walked out on me and our boys."

"She just left?" Royce responded in shock. "You must have been so disappointed and angry!"

Giff shook his head. "Disappointed, yes. Angry? Well, I was at first, but soon it occurred to me I couldn't afford to be angry. I realized if I looked for things to be angry about, there would be no end to the blame and anger. I knew my life would devolve—and I wasn't about to let that happen. My boys were counting on me. That was my focus."

Royce nodded. "Impressive."

"Well, thank you . . . but I must admit, I didn't know what to do. Out of desperation, I left Jamaica and moved with my sons to Antigua, where my brother and his wife were living. They were kind enough to let us move in with them while I found a new window washing job, which made just a bit more money—but I was still struggling. The house was small, my boys were growing, and we had all sorts of needs to be paid for."

Royce looked at Gifford with compassion and asked, "Giff, what did you do?"

The older man smiled broadly. "Enter Sir Godfrey Tillman."

Royce's puzzled look urged Gifford on. "Mr. Tillman was visiting Antigua, where he had some rental properties. He saw me cleaning windows at a coffee shop, and he just struck up a conversation with me. No one had ever done that in all my years of cleaning windows! He told me he noticed what a great job I was doing. He then asked about my family, and I guess I got a little choked up as I started telling my story. When I finished, I expected this kind stranger to just pat me on the back and say, 'Good luck.' But you know what he did?"

Royce eagerly replied, "Tell me."

"He put out his hand to shake mine, and then he said, 'Come work for me, Mr. Witherspoon. I have multiple properties with windows I wish to keep impeccably clean. You seem like the exact person for the job.' I was shocked—and he offered me five times the pay I was currently making!"

Seeing Royce's look of awe, Giff leaned back and smiled broadly. "That's exactly the way I was feeling, my friend! But the best is yet to come. From that day forward, Sir Godfrey began teaching me about his properties and how to invest in real estate. In the beginning, I knew nothing about this type of business, but I listened well, and I took a little of my pay each payday and invested it where Godfrey told me to—and he matched my investment each time. After five years, not only did I have a brand-new home for me and my boys, I also owned three rental properties!"

"What?" Royce said in disbelief.

"Yes, and the longer I stayed with Mr. Tillman's company, the more he taught me. Each time he visited Antigua, he would teach me. We were together for hours at a time, and I soaked up his lessons like a sponge."

"Ha!" Royce laughed in agreement. "I know exactly what you mean. I felt the same way when I talked with him."

Giff smiled, then calmly added, "Today, I have put both of my sons through medical school in Grenada, and I own more properties than anyone in Antigua, although almost no one knows it—which is the way I like it." He grinned.

Royce reflected on that anonymity as he thought about the young man at the hotel's front desk, who had never heard of Gifford Witherspoon when Royce asked the day before.

"What a story," Royce marveled. "But . . . you still wash windows? Surely you have enough money to buy ten window washing companies by now!" he said with a smile.

Gifford threw back his head and laughed. "Well, sure, but I love what I do." Then leaning forward as if to share a secret, he added, "My work is my offering to God. It's an honor to see these windows shine after I finish with them. Plus," he said with a wink, "you can learn an awful lot about folks by the way they treat an ordinary window washer."

Royce smiled. "I'm sure you can."

At that moment, their food arrived, and the men proceeded to enjoy every bite until their plates were clean.

"That was some seriously good Creole chicken!" Royce said with a smile.

"Yep," agreed Gifford. "Now I understand what all the fuss was about!"

The waitress noted the men's enjoyment as she walked up, nodding in approval at the clean plates. "Didn't like that at all, did you, gentlemen?" she said with a playful grin.

Royce smiled and sarcastically replied, "Nah . . . I might have to try again later and see if the next round is any better." The trio laughed, then Royce paid her for the meal, for which Gifford thanked him profusely.

"Now, Royce, if you'll excuse me, I must get back to work. These windows need a little extra tender loving care," he said with a grin. "But I do have something for you. Walk with me over to my truck."

The two men walked about twenty yards to Giff's old pickup. "She's a beauty, isn't she?" Giff said. "Ten years, and never a bit of trouble! That's more than I can say for my ex-wife," he added with a chuckle. Opening the passenger door, he reached into the glove compartment and pulled out an envelope from underneath a stack of papers. "I believe this is for you, my friend. It's from Sir Godfrey."

With that, Gifford Witherspoon tipped his cap, stuck out his hand, and shook Royce's hand heartily. "Until we meet again, Royce. It's been a pleasure."

"The pleasure was mine, for sure," replied Royce as he accepted the envelope.

Gifford smiled and walked back over to the window he had been working on, and Royce started the short trek to the hotel beach to sit down and open his latest "treasure hunt" update. Once again, as with Dianne LeCraw, Royce had the distinct feeling he and Giff had much in common.

CHAPTER 10

When he arrived at the beach, Royce sat under a large palm tree and took a moment to reflect on his time thus far in Antigua. The last and only other time he had been to the Caribbean was on a cruise he had taken six years before, at the encouragement of friends, shortly after his wife had passed away. Royce thought back on the voyage and how therapeutic that week in the warm climate had been for him. He closed his eyes, and his mind drifted off, replaying those melancholy scenes with all the different personalities on board. . .

It was April, and it was the last week of the season that cruise lines frequented Caribbean waters. The changing tourist season would then send boats on journeys far north to Alaska, Vancouver, and the like, leaving the tropics far behind. Winter was turning to spring in the cruise world—just as Royce hoped would eventually happen in his own painful life.

In the first few days of the journey, he noted how each passenger, like himself, was following their own path. Many seemed to be trying to escape something, and many seemed to be trying to find something. But everyone's story was unique.

There was the father with his young adult son, trying desperately to reconnect after a lifetime of the dad "not being there," as the young man softly put it.

There were the two old veterans who were sharing stories of how they snuck behind enemy lines and stole supplies for their troops during the war so many years ago, when they were barely out of their teens. In the safety and warmth of the ship's open-air deck, they raised their glasses of whiskey and belly-laughed at the memory.

Then there was his next-door neighbor on the ship, an elderly woman who was standing outside her balloon-adorned cabin door, struggling and grimacing as she attempted to pick up two of the balloons that had fallen to the floor. As Royce picked them up for her, she smiled broadly and proclaimed, "I have to get these back on the door right away. The captain gave them to us to celebrate sixty years for my husband and me, you know."

Royce heartily congratulated her, then her husband stepped out the door and reassuringly touched the woman's frail shoulder, smiling back at Royce.

So many stories. . .

The mothers bonding over conversations with their daughters. . .

The widows and widowers standing apart, staring quietly and pensively at the passing sea. Royce knew those expressions only too well from his own experience of being in their shoes. . .

Then there was the sacred feeling of the trip—as with all his travels. Status, age, ethnicity, religion, political differences seemed to matter little in those travels, and especially on this trip. He felt that they were all on the journey together, hoping that the rushing waters would carry away a few of their struggles, and that the palm trees and sandy shores ahead represented better days to come.

And then, as the ship finally headed out on its last leg of the trip home, that's exactly what was happening.

Royce saw the grown son embrace his father as tears trickled down both of their smiling faces.

The widows and widowers had gotten acquainted and were now sharing warm coffee and warmer conversations.

The old veterans had returned to their same spot, and now had fallen peacefully asleep, their two glasses of half-finished whiskey still firmly in their grasp, much like the pistols they had clutched in their early trips behind enemy lines.

The balloons were safely returned to their place on his neighbor's door.

These poignant scenes reminded Royce that the harshness of winter was indeed fading into a hopeful spring—and what he had seen on the journey helped him feel confident that the same would someday happen for him, as well. . .

Just then, a loud crashing wave interrupted Royce's nostalgic reverie, whereupon he sat up quickly and shook his head, trying to mentally regroup. After a few seconds, he managed to clear his mind of the cobwebs, and it occurred to him it was time to get to the matter at hand: the letter Gifford Witherspoon had given him.

Opening the envelope, Royce paused as he read the first two words: *Dear Royce*. He wondered how in the world Godfrey had miraculously managed to get the envelopes to these people well ahead of time, with Royce's name on the letters inside, when he had passed shortly after meeting Royce!

Right then, he stopped himself as Godfrey's words again popped into his mind: "*Just allow it to unfold.*"

Royce laughed, looked upward, and said aloud, "Ok, ok, I get it, Godfrey!"

He continued reading. . .

You have now met another amazing person.

What Gifford Witherspoon likely didn't share with you is that he is one of the most magnanimous men in all of Antigua. As his income grew, so did his faith, including his trust that there is—and always will be—plenty of money to go around. This belief became the guiding light in his life. With great humility, he decided to share as much as he could to help as many people as possible. As in my own life, I noticed that the more money he gave away, the more money he seemed to have. His determination to succeed not only in his window washing business, but also to grow his real estate holdings, was inspiring. His persistence was unrelenting—just as The Six Principles of Sacred Power *spoke of. I am grateful indeed to have met him, and to have watched him raise his sons to be great people who, like Giff, have helped others live happier and more fulfilled lives.*

Now, it is time to move on to the next person on your journey. Elizabeth Watson is a lovely woman who lives in St. Philip Parish in the village of Willikies, on the northeast part of the island. Her home is only about thirty minutes from Somerset Point, and you'll find the scenery along the way to be quite beautiful.

Press on, Royce!

Godfrey

Royce folded up the letter and placed it back in the envelope. He looked around, as if expecting to see someone nearby orchestrating this entire expedition, but of course there was *not* anyone else there. All he saw was a pristine Caribbean beach with tall, beautiful palm trees and a gorgeous background of sparkling blue water.

Royce tried to piece together similarities in the people he had met so far. He didn't reach a conclusion, but what he did already know was that he felt a deep connection with each of them—*almost as if he had known them before this time in Antigua*. Scratching his head in thought, he stood up to get underway for the next part of his trek.

After walking back to his room, Royce gathered his belongings and headed down to the front desk to check out. Once he arrived in the lobby, he saw the same clerk at the desk, and the young man welcomed him with a smile.

"Checking out?" he asked cheerfully.

"Yes," Royce replied with a smile. "It was truly a pleasure."

The young man looked at Royce and appreciatively replied, "I'm glad to hear it, sir—and I believe your driver is waiting for you outside, whenever you're ready."

Royce nodded, paid his bill, then turned and walked out the front door. Sure enough, there was Julian once again, waiting on him with a mischievous grin.

"Ready to go, Mr. Holloway?"

Royce couldn't hide his puzzled look. "Ok, hold on . . . how did you—"

Julian stopped him and smiled. "No time to chitchat, sir. I believe we are off to Willikies, right?"

Royce laughed and shook his head in incredulity. "I'm not sure how you knew that either, my friend, but . . . yes, let's go."

"Alrighty, then," Julian said in his strong Antiguan accent. He took Royce's luggage and threw it in the back seat, then opened the passenger door and gestured for Royce to sit in the front with him. "Would you do me the honor, sir?"

"Gladly." Royce plopped down into the seat and closed the door as Julian got back in, put the car in gear, and began heading down the driveway out of the jungle.

"So, how was your visit, sir?" Julian asked.

"It was . . . amazing," Royce replied with a satisfied look.

"Yep, you never know what you'll see—or who you'll meet—at Somerset Point. It's a special place. Many would even call it a spiritual place. Every time I pick someone up from there, they seem to have had a similar type of experience as you've had. It's supremely peaceful, to say the least."

The philosophical words struck Royce as odd, coming from a man as young as Julian. But then again, it was just another example of how there was nothing "typical" about this cab driver.

At that point, Royce instinctively turned to him and said, "Julian, I have to say, I've met some extraordinary people over the last few days—and the last few years. In fact, I'm no longer even surprised when unique, wise people enter my life. And I'll admit, you are one of those people."

The young man smiled. "I take that as quite a compliment, sir." He paused briefly, as if he wasn't sure he should continue, then added, "Mr. Holloway, may I share something with you?"

Royce wondered what was coming next, but with a reassuring smile, he replied, "Of course, feel free."

Julian took a deep breath, then said cautiously, "Mr. Holloway . . . I was Sir Godfrey's personal driver."

Royce couldn't help but blurt out, "What?!"

A smile came across Julian's face. "Yes, sir, some of the best years of my life."

"That's fantastic, Julian! So, you knew Sir Godfrey well, I assume?"

"I should say so," he said, now chuckling at Royce's obvious surprise. "In the early years when Sir Godfrey had first arrived on the island, he felt the need to keep a low profile, as you likely know. It was my job to get him to the places he needed to go, as discreetly as possible—and that's exactly what I did. After Antigua was granted independence from England, he was able to lower his guard and have fewer concerns about his safety, but he kept me as his driver."

"Amazing," Royce said, still reeling from Julian's admission.

"I learned so much about life from being around him. My father passed away when I was nineteen, so I took a job as a cab driver to help cover the expenses for my mom and me. I met Sir Godfrey when I received a call from Suzanne Dismont one day; she needed a driver to take him into town. Of course, I didn't know anything about Sir Godfrey's renown at the time, but when I picked him up, we had the most incredible conversation on our short trip to his destination. It was as if he immediately understood me and my struggles on a deep level."

Royce was infatuated with the young man's story, and he continued to listen intently.

"Sir Godfrey then asked me to be his personal driver—under the condition that I would not tell anyone. The funny thing is, I look back and can't believe he trusted me with such important, sensitive information. I was just a kid! But I am so grateful he did give me a chance. The longer I was around him, the more spiritual and personally powerful I felt myself becoming. I am literally a different person from being with him all those years. I now believe in myself and my abilities, at a level which I never knew I was capable of before."

Royce smiled in an understanding way. "It makes sense now—your intuition, your demeanor, your deep insights. . ."

Julian stopped him. "Mr. Holloway, if I could be so bold, I see those same things in you. I noticed it quickly after I picked you up at Sir Godfrey's home. I know you are an inspirational writer, but . . . there is something else about you. Sir Godfrey left me a note before he went on his last trip and asked me to take care of someone that would be coming to visit in a few months. I knew immediately I would help—and I was happy to do so—yet I had no idea he would never be coming back."

Royce nodded and placed a reassuring hand on the young man's shoulder. "I understand, Julian. I only spent a short time with Godfrey, but it was all the time I needed to know that he was a spiritual giant. He helped me fully see the kind of person I could be—just like he obviously did with you. I think the best thing we can do to honor him is to use our God-given gifts and innate skills with compassion and trust. You certainly seem to be doing that."

Julian seemed relieved to hear Royce's words of affirmation. He managed a smile, then looked Royce in the eyes. "Thank you, Mr. Holloway. I am grateful for those words; I needed to hear them."

Royce smiled as Julian added, "Now sir, let's get you to your next destination. I have a feeling there's another very special person you need to meet. . ."

CHAPTER 11

Royce and Julian continued talking as they drove northeast through the Antiguan countryside. Their conversation ranged from fun, simple banter to deeply insightful discussions about life. It was clear that Julian's connection to Godfrey Tillman had led to some powerful absorption of the Six Principles' concepts—although Julian, of course, had no knowledge of the actual book.

At one point on their trek, Royce pointed, astonished. "Julian, I've never seen so many donkeys on the side of the road in my life!"

Julian laughed. "Yes, they're all over the country! Not sure where they came from originally, but they're obviously here to stay. I think they like the place as much as the tourists do," he said with a smile.

Royce grinned broadly and agreed as he continued to enjoy the attractions along the way: more hibiscus growing wildly, beautiful waterfalls, and countless pineapple fields.

A few minutes later, Julian announced, "Almost there, Mr. Holloway. We've just entered Saint Philip Parish. It's where I was born," he said proudly.

"Beautiful place indeed," Royce replied as he took in the scenery.

As Julian nodded in agreement, he pointed up ahead to the left about five hundred feet. Perched just off the road on a small hill was a quaint English cottage made of stone and topped with a thatched roof. "That's Miss Watson's house."

Royce looked at Julian and smiled. "I'm not going to ask how you knew I was meeting Miss Watson. Your time with Godfrey tells me all I need to know about your spiritual gifts."

Julian grinned. "Well, I suppose you're right about that. Then again, Godfrey told me we all have these abilities. Funny thing is, I was never able to use them before I met him. I've never quite understood how. . ."

Royce interrupted, "So, do you know Miss Watson?"

"Yes, sir, I know her from growing up here. Amazing woman. I would say she is one of the happiest people in Antigua. You will enjoy your time with her—I'm sure of that."

One of the happiest people in Antigua? Now Royce *really* wanted to meet this woman. With those words, the cab had reached Elizabeth's home, about a hundred feet off the main street. Julian parked the car, smiled, and bid Royce goodbye. "Pick you up when you're ready, Mr. Holloway."

This time, Royce didn't ask questions. "Ok, Julian, I'll see you then—whenever 'then' is!" Royce chuckled, opened the door of the cab, and waved goodbye as he stepped out. Smiling, Julian quickly reached back, grabbed Royce's travel bag, and tossed it gently to him. Royce caught the bag and closed the door, then Julian backed the car down the driveway to find his next fare of the day.

Royce admired the little bungalow before him. The perfectly cut stone and well-manicured yard reminded him in some ways of Maya's cottage back in Georgia. Walking up to the front porch, Royce thought—as he often did—about those times he'd spent with his mentor, and how she had changed his life. He reminisced about the people he had met since that time, and he thought about the people he never would have met if it hadn't been for Maya. He couldn't imagine it—especially the thought of not ever having met Godfrey Tillman.

Royce's nostalgic thoughts were interrupted by the front door of the cottage opening just as he began walking up the stairs of the porch. The attractive gray-haired woman who stepped out to greet him was likely in her early sixties, and she had a confident yet kind presence about her. With a beautiful smile and a charming British accent, she asked, "Can I help you?"

Royce smiled in return. "I'm a friend of Sir Godfrey's. The name is Royce Holloway."

As if she knew him, the woman opened her arms wide and embraced Royce. It reminded him of the hugs one would get—and give—back home in the South. "I'm Elizabeth Watson," she said with a smile. "Do come in, Mr. Holloway."

Royce nodded and stepped inside. "Thank you, ma'am."

Entering the home, Royce was impressed by the impeccable decor. It reminded him of the story Maya had shared five years ago, about the man with the perfectly organized home in Bangladesh, which she and her father had visited. Maya had talked about what an example of precision the inside of that home seemed to be—everything in its place—and Elizabeth's home was the same way.

Gesturing toward a beautiful antique chair, Elizabeth cheerfully said, "Have a seat, Royce. I'll get us some tea, and I just made a fresh coconut pie, which is cooling in the kitchen for a few minutes."

"Sounds great!" Royce responded enthusiastically. "I could use a little pick-me-up."

She smiled and walked into the kitchen, and as Royce continued to look around her home, he noticed a grouping of pictures of Elizabeth and a man whom Royce surmised was her husband. Each picture showed the happy couple in unique places—on a train with snow-capped mountains in the background, on a boat in Mediterranean surroundings, and even riding camels in the desert.

Returning to the room and handing Royce his tea, Elizabeth saw him admiring the various pictures. Apparently feeling comfortable enough to open up to him, she smiled and offered softly, "We loved to travel."

Royce nodded, and noting her tone, followed up gently. "Those look like fantastic places. I'm a traveler, too."

She smiled. "The handsome gentleman in the picture was my husband, Phillip. He passed away about ten years ago, tragically. I loved him so much, and I still miss him—and our adventures—even today."

"I understand," said Royce. "My wife passed away as well; it's difficult to describe the pain."

"I'm sorry," she replied, shaking her head. "It's something I wouldn't wish upon anyone. At times, it has seemed almost unbearable. In fact, if it hadn't been for Sir Godfrey, I'm not sure I *would* have been able to bear it. He saved my life, I would say." She paused, then quickly added, "Forgive me, Mr. Holloway, you didn't come here to listen to my problems."

Royce smiled and then offered in a comforting way, "I'm grateful you would share your story with me; I'm sure we have a lot in common. If you don't mind, could you tell me more about Sir Godfrey's role in helping you? I only knew him for a short time, but he certainly helped me as well."

Looking away, Elizabeth became quiet, appearing to be deep in thought. Royce wondered if he had said something to offend her.

"I hope I didn't say something. . ."

Elizabeth shook her head and held up her hand. "On the contrary. Let me tell you about Godfrey and what he did for me."

Royce leaned in as Elizabeth began her story.

"Shortly after my husband died, I ran into Sir Godfrey at a small British grocery store tucked away off a side street in St. John's. I didn't know who he was at the time, but he spoke to me, and he had such a kind way about him. I had lost all my self-confidence after the death of Phillip, and I was a nervous wreck every day. My anxiety had increased to the point where I couldn't sleep, couldn't eat, really couldn't even carry on a conversation without trembling. I know it sounds ridiculous, but. . ."

Royce interrupted her and said softly, "I know. Social anxiety is a painful thing which I've experienced also."

Elizabeth smiled as she realized she was talking to someone who didn't judge her. "Thank you for saying that, Royce. It means a lot. Sir Godfrey said something similar, and just the fact that someone didn't tell me what I *should* do was incredibly refreshing. He simply listened—like you obviously do very well."

"He was the best at that," Royce chimed in with a smile.

"It was out of my comfort zone, but after talking with him in the store for a few moments, I asked if he would join me for a cup of tea sometime, which he kindly accepted for the next day. For some reason—I'm not sure why—I felt he could help me.

"Sir Godfrey came to my home, and he could immediately sense that I was struggling with so much fear. I remember the conversation almost word for word. At one point, he put down his tea, looked me squarely in the eyes and said with that big Godfrey smile, 'Elizabeth, what kind of person do you desire to be? What traits do you wish to have?' I thought the question odd, but nonetheless, I quickly said, 'I want to be a confident, kind, loving person who has the strength to face anything life throws at me.' I paused, feeling a bit awkward, wondering if I had said too much. . ."

Royce's eyes showed his riveted interest as she continued the story.

"Godfrey looked at me in a reassuring way and said, 'Then that is the type of person you *shall* be.'

"My puzzled look apparently showed him I didn't understand, and so he continued, 'Elizabeth, what can truly keep you from being a confident, kind, loving, determined person?'

" 'Well, fear, I suppose,' I said.

"Godfrey smiled, shook his head, and replied, 'My dear, anything worthwhile involves fear.'

"So I said, 'Guilt and regret, then.'

" 'Certainly not,' he countered. 'They are both imposters. Try again.' He grinned.

"I paused and said, 'Sir Godfrey, I am afraid if I try, I may fall deeply into the dreadful abyss of failure.'

"Godfrey paused, then looked at me with those piercing blue eyes, and calmly said, 'Yes, you may. Then again, you may instead soar mightily into the magnificent sky of unlimited possibilities—especially if you *believe* that is what will happen. In my opinion, that is *exactly* what will happen.

Elizabeth hesitated for a few seconds, then said, "Right then, I had an epiphany. I knew everything I wanted was within my grasp—if I chose to believe it. I began telling myself that I *would* be the person I wanted to be. Then, I started reaching out to help others, which took my mind off my own problems. Funny, the more I did that, the more I realized how much happier I was. I also became aware of how much other people needed to be listened to, and how many people had challenges even greater than mine—even though it had felt as if I was all alone with my problems.

"I began volunteering, and I looked for ways I could reach out and give to others. Sometimes it was monetary, sometimes it was my time or my talent . . . but the key question I constantly asked myself was—and still is today—'What can I give now?'

Royce nodded and smiled. "There was no one to better teach about generosity than Sir Godfrey. He was truly a master. I know my life is much richer because of what he taught me about dealing with and helping others."

Elizabeth nodded in agreement. "It's true, Royce. Also, Godfrey seemed to have so much confidence, and when I asked him about that confidence, he replied with an answer that I will never forget. He said, 'Elizabeth, my secret to feeling confident is to do everything I can to help others find their own confidence.'"

Royce smiled in approval as Elizabeth continued.

"A few days after that conversation with Sir Godfrey, I was sitting in a café, and I saw something unfold which cemented his words in my heart."

Royce tilted his head with an intrigued look as Elizabeth carried on with her story.

"While I was sitting at the counter, I watched a frail, humble woman, who appeared to be around seventy years old, work 'magic.' She was a member of the cooking staff; she wasn't a manager or an owner, but I did understand she was a shift supervisor. She was a gentle and magnetic leader who I soon came to realize earned respect through love, not out of fear.

"As I sat at the counter for thirty minutes or so, having lunch and then sipping my tea, I saw team members come to her like she was Mother Teresa. She would put her arm around them, listen briefly to their situation or problem—whether it was personal or business. Then she would smile and encourage them. Finally, she would hug them, and they would move on. Oh, and she also had a wonderful work ethic! In fact, at one point I saw a server come up and report to her, 'Everything is ready for the next shift. It's perfect; I don't want to ever let you down.' Upon hearing that, the older woman smiled, placed her hand on the young woman's shoulder, and quietly said, 'You never have. Thank you, honey.'

"And I noticed the manager of the restaurant wasn't threatened by the esteem in which the staff clearly held this woman. Quite the contrary—the manager seemed to be grateful for the compassionate glue that the matronly supervisor provided."

Royce nodded as he envisioned the scene.

Elizabeth added with a smile, "Royce, right then, something clicked, and I fully understood that wherever we are, whatever we do, whatever our role or our situation, no matter how painful or difficult things seem, we have the power to step out of our own worries and insecurities to touch and change other peoples' lives—maybe, in a small way, to even change the world. It's what this woman was doing, and I deeply wanted to do the same thing."

Elizabeth paused, then concluded, "Ever since hearing Sir Godfrey's words that day, and then seeing that woman's selfless compassion, I haven't worried about the way I am perceived. I simply focus on using my gifts to empower others. In fact, I sometimes spend several hours per day calling friends or writing letters or looking for ways I can help. The ironic thing is that if you asked people in this community about me, they would likely say I seem to be a person who hasn't a care in the world. Little do they know that it took Sir Godfrey to help me regain that confidence and poise that had been pushed down so deep inside me."

Royce sat quietly for a few seconds, taking her words in. Finally, he said, "It seems paradoxical, but the more we do for others, the more we are doing for ourselves, too."

Elizabeth smiled. "I can vouch for that. I used to worry that people might not like me, or they might misunderstand me, or they might unfairly judge me. Now I seldom worry about what others think of me, because I'm too busy thinking about how I can help make the world a better place. That's my focus, and if there are people who don't like that, or don't like me—and I'm sure those folks are out there—then that's ok. I guess you can't please everyone."

"Yes!" Royce exclaimed. "Along those same lines, Godfrey reminded me that if we're worried about pleasing everyone, we're going to become such approval addicts that the constant need to please people will crowd out the joy that comes from selfless giving."

"Beautifully said, Royce. I agree, and I would add one more thing that Sir Godfrey taught me. . ."

Royce listened intently to this wise woman as she continued, "Godfrey believed that when our lives are winding down, one of the things we look back on is how much—or how little—we did for others. I believe that, too. Don't get me wrong; I'm not saying that we should be keeping track of our good deeds. What I mean is that every time we do something unselfishly for others, we are reinforcing our trust. We're reminding ourselves that we know our needs will be taken care of, and so we are able to help those who may not have learned that lesson yet. Then, the more trust we have, the happier and more carefree we will be, and the more depth and impact our giving will have in the lives of others. It's a powerful 'secret' to happiness, and the beauty of it is, we can choose to follow this path at any time, and this secret will never let us down."

Thinking back on Julian's comment about Elizabeth's joyful spirit, he chipped in, "Well, you certainly do seem as happy as I've heard you are! It's been an honor to talk with you."

"Thank you, Royce, but I have to say, I'm not sure I would have understood this lesson without having spent time with Sir Godfrey. I could never thank him enough." Elizabeth stood up and said with a smile, "Now, how about we go get a piece of that coconut pie?"

Royce grinned and followed her into the kitchen, where she cut him a hearty slice of the delicious dessert. The two of them sat down, and Royce gobbled up the pie like a famished man. After a little more conversation, he pushed back from the table and commented, "Well, I suppose I should be on my way." Laughing, he added, "I'm sure my cab driver is waiting on me."

Elizabeth smiled and said with a perplexed expression, "But you haven't even called one!"

Royce shook his head and smiled. "That's a whole different story, but let's just say, Sir Godfrey taught *him* a thing or two as well."

With an understanding look, Elizabeth stood up and walked over to a small desk just outside the kitchen, reached into the top drawer, and pulled out an envelope. "Speaking of Sir Godfrey . . . this is for you, Royce. He asked me to hold onto it until the 'right person' came along. He said I would know who that would be—and I have no doubt that person is you."

Royce stood up to receive the envelope from her. "Thank you so much, Elizabeth. I'll always remember this conversation. I'm very grateful."

"It was truly my pleasure," she replied as she escorted Royce to the front door.

Stepping outside, Royce saw Julian with his window rolled down, smiling as if to say, "Well, I'm here—what did you expect?" Royce couldn't help but chuckle.

Walking to the cab, he looked back a final time and saw Elizabeth waving goodbye. "Safe travels!" she called out.

Royce waved back as he ducked into the car and nodded hello to Julian. Then eagerly opening the envelope to reveal its precious contents, Royce took a long, deep breath as they pulled away toward the unknown next stop on this mysterious and extraordinary journey. . .

CHAPTER 12

As Julian exited the driveway onto the main street in Willikies, he glanced over to ask about the visit with Elizabeth, then noticed Royce deeply engrossed in the message inside the envelope.

With a furrowed brow and great anticipation, Royce began reading to himself:

Dear Royce,

I trust your visit to the little hamlet was quite rewarding. Elizabeth Watson is one of the finest women I have ever had the pleasure of meeting. Her struggles, as for many of us, were heartbreaking, yet she used those battles to become a stronger, wiser, more compassionate person—and a happier person, too.

Elizabeth was able to rise above the challenges she faced, and yet so many people don't realize they are innately capable of doing that same thing. Instead, they live their lives in a quietly desperate state of simply hoping things will somehow get better. Royce, like Elizabeth, you can continue to help people see what they are capable of—and this world will be a better place because of that.

You are getting closer to your journey's ultimate destination. However, there are still more people to meet. Your next stop will be a place that you may find interesting—and I know *the person you meet will impress you. He is an exceptional young man with a compelling story. His name is Roberto Castillo, and you will find him at 104 Western Cape Road in Five Islands Village.*

Enjoy your journey, Royce. . .

Godfrey

Royce looked up from the letter. "My friend, we are headed cross-country; thankfully, Antigua is a small island! This time, we're going to a place called Five Islands Village."

Julian glanced at him and smiled. "Going to see Roberto, huh?"

Royce laughed. "Julian, you remind me of my friend Maya; she used to finish my sentences. But yes, you are correct. How did you know we were headed to see Roberto Castillo? Is this guy the only person in the village or something?"

Julian chuckled. "Well, I'll say this: he certainly is a well-known person in the village. Maybe the best-known resident, aside from Sir Vivian, who also lives there."

Royce's look showed he was clearly shocked. Since he had been on the island, he had heard incredible stories from the locals about Sir Vivian Richards. "Wait . . . you're telling me Roberto is almost as well known as the greatest cricket player ever to come out of Antigua? This guy must be *really* special."

"Yes, indeed. But I won't spoil your visit. You can find out more about him for yourself," Julian said with a grin. "Five Islands Village it is, my friend."

Royce smiled and leaned back in the passenger seat to get comfortable for their trip across the country to the west coast. As he did, the prospect of a little extra time together seemed to encourage Julian to engage in some conversation. Hesitating briefly, he then asked, "Royce, is this your first time in Antigua?"

"Yes, but I can tell it won't be my last," Royce responded with a grin. "It's absolutely beautiful—in fact, it's one of the prettiest places I've seen in the world!"

Julian wistfully shook his head. "All my life, I have wanted to travel. Hearing Sir Godfrey talk about the places he had been and the people he'd been able to spend time with just made me want to pick up and go. Tell me about some of the people you've met."

"I have many wonderful memories—and each person I've met seemed to have something to teach me," Royce said with a nostalgic look. He gazed out the window as the tropical scenery rolled by, appearing to be deep in thought. Finally, he broke the silence. "There is *one* person—and the lesson he taught me—that really stands out. . ."

Julian's look of anticipation urged Royce on.

"When I was in my early twenties, I spent some time playing the men's professional tennis circuit—enough to know that it's a lot of fun, but a really hard way to make a living," he said with a grin. "One stop on the tour was the mystical country of India, and it was there I met a well-seasoned traveler who shared some poignant words with me that I will never forget."

Julian smiled and settled in as Royce continued. "I was on a break from my competition in Bombay, which is now Mumbai, near the seaside state of Goa, when our paths crossed on a deserted beach. He, too, was an American, and his gray hair and deeply lined, tanned face led me to believe he was probably in his seventies. When we met, as with many world travelers, our connection was an immediate one. We had a lively, engaging conversation about the places we'd been and the experiences we'd had during our travels. But when I asked him where his favorite place he'd ever visited was, he paused, his eyes became misty, and he softly said this. . .

" 'Royce, travel is wonderful. I've seen the colossal pyramids in Egypt, the rugged and mysterious Outback in Australia, and the beautiful beaches in Thailand. But at this point in my life, I now understand that the real treasure in life does not lie in any one place. It's not just gulping down the visits to faraway, exotic destinations. It's learning to be grateful wherever I am—whether I am traveling or not.'

"He continued, 'It occurred to me one day that I had wasted much of my life always looking ahead, waiting for my next great adventure, instead of making my next great adventure out of wherever I was at the time—including savoring the 'little' things, like simple moments with those I love. I missed so much of who and what was around me that I will never be able to get back...' "

Julian seemed entranced as Royce continued with his story.

"After a little more conversation, the traveler began gathering his belongings, and as we raised our drinks to toast family and friends back in the United States one last time, I became acutely aware of the warm breeze gently blowing in off the Arabian Sea. Even with that warmth, I felt a chill go through me as I suddenly sensed how deeply I missed my faraway little Georgia home and the people I loved.

"As we said our goodbyes—he was headed to Africa, and I would soon go back to Bombay—I think we both realized what a spiritual time this short afternoon had been for each of us. I decided to stay a little longer on the beach, and I relaxed back into the soft, brown sand. Watching him fade up the coastline into the seemingly endless line of majestic palm trees, I knew I would be bringing home a powerful lesson from that chance meeting in India: if we spend too much time focusing on where we want to be in the future, we may get there only to realize that the future destination we really wanted . . . is now distantly and irretrievably lost in the past."

Julian smiled gently and gave an approving look. "Ah, yes, the mark of an excellent traveler, and a wise man, always learning from others. That is a beautiful story, and a valuable lesson, sir."

Royce seemed lost in thought for a moment, then he replied, "It's interesting, Julian, every time I think about that time on the beach with the traveler in India, I think about the times in my own life that I have missed the moments that are so precious. Even though I'm acutely aware of the brevity of life, I still must remind myself to stop and appreciate wherever I am and whoever I'm with. Each time I do that, I realize how blessed we all are."

"No doubt about it, Royce. Thank you for reminding me as well," Julian said with a smile.

After that, the two men sat quietly for a while, each of them pondering the conversation as the miles ticked off and more of the spectacular Antiguan scenery whizzed by.

Ten minutes later, they passed an old sugar mill, one of many that dotted the island landscape.

"I heard the British used those mills in the production of sugar starting way back in the early sixteen hundreds. How many of the facilities are still around?" asked Royce.

Julian thought for a few seconds. "One hundred and twelve was the last count I heard. Of course, most all of them have been reduced to ruins, except for a few in places like Betty's Hope, which have been restored for historic purposes." His demeanor became solemn as he added, "That period from the sixteen hundreds up to emancipation in the eighteen hundreds was a crimson stain on the fabric of Antigua. So many people died from the horrific treatment they received while being forced to work on the sugar plantations as slaves."

Royce shook his head. "As you know, we had our own terrible times in the US. I can't fathom how people ever could have thought slavery was justifiable. It's just unreal."

Julian nodded somberly.

Just then, the mood changed as Julian spotted a sign pointing to Western Cape Road in their destination of Five Islands Village. "Ah, we're here, Royce! Your stop is just around this next corner."

Exiting onto an inconspicuous little side street, then doing a sharp U-turn around a grouping of large, lush palm trees, Julian and Royce quickly found themselves in front of a row of three whitewashed Caribbean-style buildings, one on the far end proclaiming the address: 104 Western Cape Road. Above the address was a small, tastefully done metal sign, painted turquoise and yellow, with the words CASTILLO'S GYM emblazoned in black letters.

Staring up at the sign, Julian smiled. "Well, I believe this is the place. It's four o'clock now, so I'll leave and come back around six. That should be about right."

Julian grinned as Royce jokingly rolled his eyes. "I suppose that *will* be about right, based on our track record so far."

Royce got out of the cab and walked a few steps to the entrance, whereupon a handsome, trim, brown-eyed young man of about thirty opened the door for him.

"Welcome to Castillo's Gym!" he said with a broad smile. "My name is Roberto, and I am honored to have you here."

Royce was taken aback, not just by the overwhelming kindness of the young man, but also by the fact that he *was* such a young man. "Hi, I'm Royce Holloway from America. So, you're the owner of the gym?"

"I am indeed," he said with a grin, sensing Royce's surprise.

As Royce stepped inside and looked around the facility, he estimated that the size of the space was around twenty-five thousand square feet, and it was beautiful. Every piece of equipment was neatly in its place, the whole club was impeccably clean, and a great variety of people were working out throughout the gym. It was a veritable beehive of positive energy.

"Looks like you have a lot of happy people here," Royce offered.

"My members are the best," Roberto said, looking out over the facility. "People sometimes come from an hour away just to be here, even though there are plenty of other closer places to choose from. It's not about the exercise equipment—although you can see we have plenty of that. It's because they feel valued and appreciated here. I know the name of every person in the building right now, and I consider each person to be not just a member, but a friend," he said proudly.

"You know, I believe you," Royce agreed with a smile. "Speaking of friends, I believe we have one in common."

Roberto's quizzical look led Royce to continue.

"Sir Godfrey Tillman. Before he passed, he had suggested that I come see you."

Roberto's look went from puzzlement to one of elation as he exclaimed, "Sir Godfrey was one of the greatest men I ever met! He changed my life forever!"

"That seems to be a theme," Royce said with a laugh.

Roberto paused, looked briefly around the gym, then calmly motioned to Royce. "Come back into my office, Mr. Holloway. I would like to share something with you. . ."

CHAPTER 13

Royce followed Roberto down a long, narrow hallway, then the gym owner turned the corner and opened a door that led into a large office. As the two men entered the room, Royce was impressed with the orderliness, but even more so with the positive vibe he felt in the room—just like in the gym itself. On the walls were pictures of people participating in a variety of fitness competitions: runners, martial artists, boxers, and quite a few bodybuilders. One picture in particular caught Royce's eye: a bodybuilding competitor who looked to be in his early twenties. The young man was in magnificent condition and wore a medal around his neck, and he looked a lot like Roberto.

"Hey, the guy in this photograph, is that . . . you?"

Roberto smiled sheepishly and replied with a laugh, "Yes, sir, guilty as charged! That was back in my power training days. I don't have any other pictures like that displayed, because I don't want people to think I'm, well, you know . . . a 'meathead,' as they say."

Royce grinned. "Ah, I get it—might seem a little intimidating to your typical club members."

"Correct," Roberto said with an easy smile.

"So, has fitness always been a part of your life? I mean, I can tell that you're still in great shape. What about when you were a youth?"

"Well, I suppose that's a perfect lead-in to the story I would like to share with you," Roberto replied. "It relates to our friend Sir Godfrey."

Royce's look of intrigue wasn't lost on Roberto as the young man reached into the top drawer of his desk, pulled out a five-by-seven photograph, and began his story. "This was me when I was fourteen years old," he said, seemingly embarrassed, turning the picture around for Royce to see.

Royce had to hide his surprise. Expecting to simply see a younger version of Roberto's current physique and confident attitude, he instead saw a timid-looking boy who appeared almost emaciated.

Trying to sooth the man's obvious discomfort, Royce offered with an understanding smile, "I wasn't exactly a prime physical specimen myself. For a young boy, I know how difficult it is to be so thin. It's embarrassing because other boys can often judge you as being weak."

Roberto nodded. "Yes, and growing up here, I was already different. My parents moved to Antigua from Spain when I was just twelve. My father came here to work as a geological consultant for the government, assessing the fault lines in this part of the Caribbean. As you can see, I don't look very Antiguan." Roberto managed a forced smile.

"But if you add onto that the fact that I was so skinny, I became a prime target for being bullied. Every day for my first two years of school, I was picked on and even physically beaten. My dad was often gone for work, but even when he was here, my parents couldn't do anything to stop it. At home, I would just lock myself in my room and cry. It must have been horrible for them to see their child so distraught, and it was beyond depressing for me going through it. But then. . ."

Roberto paused as if to catch his breath and regain his composure. Royce sat quietly, waiting to hear what would come next and feeling a deep compassion for the young man.

"Then this happened . . . or should I say, *he* happened," he said with a broad smile. Just then, Roberto produced a framed picture the same size as the other one he had shown Royce. Royce immediately recognized the older man standing next to young Roberto; it was Godfrey Tillman.

"Sir Godfrey," Royce said with a knowing smile. "Even though the picture is years old, I would recognize him anywhere. But what. . ."

Roberto blurted out, "Yes! I told you he changed my life—he really did. Maybe even *saved* my life."

Royce leaned back in his chair, listening intently as Roberto continued. "One day, I was out with my father, collecting some soil samples on a beach near Nelson's Dockyard. Sir Godfrey happened to be out walking, and he saw us and became interested in what my father was doing. After about thirty minutes of conversation, he invited us to a local restaurant for lunch. It turns out the restaurant was located inside a commercial building Sir Godfrey owned."

"Yes," Royce chimed in, "I didn't realize until recently that Sir Godfrey owned so much real estate here."

Roberto shrugged. "He did. But for security reasons—and likely also because he was so humble—only a few people knew it, for many years."

Royce smiled as Roberto continued his heartfelt story.

"Anyway, when we finished lunch, Sir Godfrey gave us a tour of the building. In the back part of the complex, there was a workout area. Sir Godfrey was a big believer in health and fitness, and he had the gym built so his tenants could use it—free of charge. When I saw that space, my eyes must have gotten huge. Sir Godfrey looked at me and asked if I would like to try some exercises. I was terrified, but I nodded and said yes."

Royce watched Roberto become misty-eyed as he seemed to be reliving that time. "It was as if Sir Godfrey knew what I was going through at school. He set me up on a piece of equipment, showed me how to do a simple exercise, then smiled and confidently said, 'Young man, I think you could be very good at this. Feel free to come here any time you like, as my guest.' Whether he knew what was going on with me somehow, or whether he was just being kind, his words at that moment began my transformational journey.

"Every day after school, I would walk two miles to his gym, and I would work out. At first, I didn't know what I was doing, but I *did* know that something about me was changing. Sir Godfrey even had a professional trainer come in and help me—for free! I started getting stronger. In fact, within six months, I was the strongest boy in my school.

"One day, one of the bullies came up to me and threatened me. Looking back, I realize it was a turning point. As usual, he put his finger in my face and made fun of me. All the times before that, I would just cower, or turn and run. That day, I grabbed his hand and began squeezing it with a great deal of force. I looked him in the eyes and wanted to hurt him, like he had hurt me. But then, after several seconds of seeing the fear in his face, I thought about how Mr. Tillman would not want me to hurt the bully, or anyone else. I let his hand go, pushed him away from me, and simply stared as he ran away. After that, not only did no one pick on me ever again, but the former bullies begged me to tell them what I had done to get so strong. Of course, I never did." Roberto winked.

"Incredible," was all Royce could muster.

"Yes, it was. Occasionally, Sir Godfrey would come by when I was training in the gym, and he would encourage me. 'You've made quite the improvements, my good man,' he would remark in that British accent, with a smile. 'Quite the improvements.

Concluding his story, Roberto added, "As I got a little older, I knew this was the business I wanted to be in. I wanted to make sure I could give help to anyone who needed it. I didn't want anyone to have to go through what I did. So, after college, I scraped together enough money to build a small gym—the one you're in now—and it has grown every year. Of course, as with any venture, early on there were plenty of doubters, but the bullies had prepared me well for dealing with those kinds of people. The critics of my business would laugh at me, saying, 'Roberto, you're a fool. A health club will never work here.' But Godfrey used to tell me that when people say something will never work, it typically means *they* could never make it work. Guess I got the last laugh, instead of the cynics." He grinned.

"Even up until a few months ago, Sir Godfrey would stop by, and we would have lunch together and talk about that first day we met. Like my father, Sir Godfrey was my role model."

Royce looked out the window of the office and saw that the sun was just beginning to set, and he knew it was time to get back on the road. Standing up, he looked at Roberto and said, "This place is a powerful testimony to you—and to Sir Godfrey. I'm grateful you met with me and shared your inspirational story. Now it's time for me to head to my next stop of inspiration—wherever that is."

Roberto smiled as if he understood what Royce meant. Reaching back into his desk drawer, he pulled out an envelope and handed it to Royce. "Maybe this will give you some guidance. Sir Godfrey dropped it off the last time he was here, and he said I would know who to give it to. Now I know."

Royce smiled broadly and accepted the envelope, then the two men walked back into the gym. Strolling across the main floor, Royce noticed how the young business owner shook hands with each of the members and called them by name, exactly as he had mentioned earlier.

As they reached the front door, Roberto opened it for Royce. "It's truly been a pleasure to share my thoughts about Sir Godfrey with you. I trust that wherever your adventure takes you, my words will have helped in some way."

Royce smiled and shrugged. "Hopefully so. Even I am not sure where this is going to take me. However, I do know that I'm a better man for having spent this time with you."

Roberto beamed.

With those final words, Royce stepped out the door and into Julian's waiting cab. As the taxi pulled away, Royce looked out the window and waved a final time to Roberto, who was still stationed attentively at the door, waiting to welcome the next guest to Castillo's Gym.

Royce took a deep breath, glanced over at Julian, then settled in, looking down at the envelope he had just been given. "Well, old buddy, let's see where we're off to next."

Julian grinned as his passenger opened the envelope with great excitement. As tired as Royce was, the quest to find Mr. Gandhi's elusive copy of *The Six Principles of Sacred Power* continued to pump adrenaline through him.

He took out the letter and began reading to himself:

Dear Royce,

Did you enjoy spending time with Roberto? I have no doubt you two got along beautifully. Of all the people I know, Roberto is one of the finest examples of courage and determination. He put his mind to the way he wanted his life to be, and he stopped at nothing to attain that goal. Did he tell you that he won the World Bodybuilding Championship when he was only nineteen years old? I am guessing he didn't share that, as his strength is only exceeded by his humility. In some ways, he reminds me of you—one who was determined to rise above their challenges and help others through their work.

Now, my good man, there is one more very important person I wish for you to meet as you approach your ultimate destination. You will find Thomas Langford in an unlikely place: 265 Beacon Drive near English Harbour. However, I hope you will take the time to spend tonight at the nearby Galley Bay Inn to get some rest. It's only about ten minutes from Five Islands Village, and each time I have lodged there, I have met someone of great interest. I am sure the same will be true for you.

Travel safely,

Godfrey

With a puzzled look, Royce folded the letter back up and put it in his pocket with the other notes he had collected. His thoughts were all over the place. He realized the last leg of the journey to find the sacred book was headed back near Godfrey's residence in Shirley Heights. Could it be that the book had been right under his nose when he was at Godfrey's home? Plus, he wondered, why would Godfrey note that 265 Beacon Drive would seem an "unlikely place"?

With fatigue setting in from the last three days, Royce realized that spending the night close by, as Godfrey suggested, was a good idea. Looking over at Julian, he said, "I need to make a detour for the night. Drop me at the Galley Bay Inn, and please pick me back up tomorrow after breakfast."

Julian raised a curious eyebrow at the request, then shrugged and said, "Yes, sir," as he turned the taxi around to embark on the ten-minute drive to Galley Bay.

CHAPTER 14

The drive to Galley Bay was quick and uneventful, and when Julian let Royce out of the cab, both men were physically exhausted from the day. Royce bid him goodbye, and Julian agreed to be back in the morning for the trip to Shirley Heights.

The stone inn was quaint and well kept, and it appeared fairly small; Royce guessed there were maybe a dozen rooms, all in a row overlooking the bay. The entrance area was full of hibiscus and assorted tropical plants, and as Royce pushed the glass door open, the small lobby had a welcoming aroma of eucalyptus. Stepping up to the mahogany counter, he saw an Antiguan woman in her thirties with a pleasant smile, who cheerfully introduced herself as Yvonne. "How can I help?" she offered.

"Just a room for the night, please," Royce responded with a yawn.

"Long day, huh?" Yvonne asked with a caring tone in her voice.

"I think I could fall asleep standing up right here," Royce said with a laugh.

The young woman laughed, too. "No need for that, sir." She slid the inn's registration form to Royce. "Sign here, and I can put you in room 2, which is just about twenty yards outside the front door, to the left. You'll find the bed to be quite comfortable—much more so than sleeping here in the lobby." She handed Royce the key.

Chuckling, Royce hastily signed the document and took the key, then turned and headed back out the front door. Just as the young woman had said, the room was only a short distance away. Opening the door, he threw his bag on a chair next to a sliding glass door overlooking the bay.

A very comfortable little place, just as Godfrey said, Royce thought as he looked around the room, admiring the tasteful beach decor. But though Godfrey had also suggested that he typically ended up meeting interesting people at the inn, Royce knew there was no chance of that for *him* tonight. Taking his shoes off, he lay down on the bed to relax for just a moment, and before he knew it, he was fast asleep.

Royce slept through the night and was only awakened the next morning by a tropical bird chirping loudly outside the sliding glass door. Startled, he sat up and noticed the sun was already rising over the ocean. He glanced at his watch.

"Six thirty! I didn't know I was *that* tired," Royce said, rubbing his eyes. He jumped out of bed, then turned the water on for a shower as he began thinking of the day ahead. He wondered who he could possibly meet that would cap off this amazing parade of people who had already crossed his path in Antigua. Then he thought about the book. Would today be the day he was led to the copy of *The Six Principles of Sacred Power* he sought?

Royce showered quickly and brushed his teeth, then got dressed to start his adventure for the day. Glancing down, he noticed a small card on the nightstand with a message for guests: *JOIN US FOR A DELICIOUS BREAKFAST EACH MORNING ANY TIME FROM 7:00–10:00 A.M. IN THE LOBBY CAFE.*

Royce smiled. *Just what I need,* he thought. He turned and walked out of the room, and within a minute he was back in the small lobby, where five small round tables were now set up with white tablecloths and four aqua-colored chairs at each table. Place settings had been neatly arranged for the morning's guests, of which Royce was the first as he plopped himself into a chair.

Right on time, a young server, probably in his late twenties, arrived at the table, carrying a brown carafe on a tray. He happily asked, "Coffee, sir?"

Royce grinned. "Oh, yes, I beg of you!"

The waiter laughed. "No begging necessary, sir; I know that feeling in the morning." As the man poured the steaming brew into Royce's cup, he asked with a Hispanic accent, "First time at our inn?"

"Yes, first time at the inn—and to the island," Royce replied, taking a cautious sip of the hot coffee.

"Well, welcome!" the waiter said with a broad smile. "It's always a pleasure to have first-timers here. Where are you from, if I might ask?"

"Georgia, in the United States," Royce replied with a smile. "Ever been?"

The waiter smiled again. "Well, believe it or not, I have friends in Atlanta. They were guests of ours several years ago, and we've stayed in touch. I went and visited them just last year."

Royce nodded his approval. "Fantastic! I love Atlanta, plus we have some other wonderful places in Georgia, including the mountains and the coastal areas. In fact, I have to say I am partial to the Georgia coast; I was born there."

The waiter excitedly responded, "Outstanding! I'm always looking for new places to go. I'll put that on my bucket list."

The two men talked with great engagement, which Royce always enjoyed when he traveled. Then, after a couple moments, the waiter took Royce's order of two eggs, wheat toast, and a glass of freshly squeezed juice.

"I'll have that right out for you, sir," he said, disappearing into the kitchen just a dozen steps away.

Royce couldn't help but notice the maturity and presence the young man seemed to possess at such a young age. *Something is different about this young man—different in a good way,* Royce thought with a smile.

When he brought the breakfast out a several minutes later, Royce asked the waiter where he was from.

"Mexico," he replied proudly.

"Ah, yes, one of my favorite countries!" Royce replied with a smile.

"Yes, it is full of adventures, opportunities, and untold stories—as all of life is," the waiter said with a note of poignance.

As they got to talking more, Royce could see in this young man's eyes that his path had undoubtedly been long, and he had surely learned some deep lessons throughout his life. The longer the conversation went on, the more Royce realized just how deep these lessons really were.

At one point, the young server thoughtfully offered, "Sir, in Mexico, we have a saying: 'A man cries on top of his Ferrari.'"

When Royce asked him to elaborate on that proverb, he smiled and said, "It means that if we aren't careful, we can get so busy chasing only the material things in life that we may actually catch them. When we do, we may sadly realize that we were chasing the wrong things."

Royce nodded in agreement, and the man continued, "I'm twenty-eight years old. I've been married twice, and I've been divorced twice. I've seen success, and I've seen loss. However, even at my age, I have realized this lesson: when I look back at the end of my life, I know what will be most significant are the people I met and the great experiences I had. So," he smiled, "I've committed myself to looking for more of both—and thankfully, I seem to find them quite often."

There was a tone of gentleness and authenticity in his words that was undeniable, and Royce truly believed that this young man lived out this wise philosophy.

"Thank you for those words," Royce said gently. "They are words we could all benefit from hearing again and again."

The young man smiled and nodded. "It's an honor, sir. Now, please finish your breakfast; I have taken up too much of your time." He turned and walked back into the kitchen.

When the server returned a little while later, Royce had finished breakfast and had left a generous amount of money on the table to cover the meal and tip. He stood up to tell the man goodbye. "Thank you, my friend, I hope our paths cross again. I'm grateful to have met you. I'm Royce, by the way."

"I'm Oswaldo." He placed his hand over his heart in a gesture of gratitude. "The pleasure has been mine."

As Royce walked back toward his room to gather his belongings and check out, he looked up at the beautiful blue Caribbean sky—a perfect backdrop for the gift he had just been given of time with this remarkable young man. He also couldn't help but think about how much the young man's narrative and life lesson reminded him of the traveler's story from the beach in India so many years ago.

As if he were attempting to lock the common theme of these powerful lessons into his mind once and for all, Royce articulated aloud: "Savor the good times, weather the bad times, and realize that the truly important things in our lives are the ones that can't ever be bought or sold."

Royce packed his bag, walked over to the lobby, and checked out of the Galley Bay Inn, then stepped outside to meet his waiting driver for the final stop on his mystical journey.

CHAPTER 15

Hopping into the taxi, Royce noticed how much more refreshed Julian looked.

"Wow, buddy, you got a good night's sleep too, I see!"

"I had no idea how tired I was," Julian said, shaking his head. "But I am ready to roll today!" he added with a grin.

Royce smiled and shared the address with him. "We're headed to 265 Beacon Drive near English Harbour."

Julian paused, then asked cautiously, "Did you say *265 Beacon Drive . . . ?*"

Royce checked the address again. "Yep, according to my notes."

"Well," said Julian with a laugh. "Hope you've got your waders on! That's Redonda Island; it's the address of the lighthouse. I took Mr. Tillman to the dock at English Harbour many times, so he could take a boat over there to visit a friend. It's just about fifteen minutes offshore . . . but it's definitely Redonda Island, and there's not much to it—well, unless you like old lighthouses."

Royce's perplexed look was quickly picked up on by Julian. "I'm sure there's a reason. Let's go find out. It's a forty-five-minute cross-country trip to English Harbour from here, but it's a straight shot, and I'm up for an adventure if you are," Julian said with a big smile.

"Here we go, my friend!" Royce fired back.

As they began the trip, Julian looked over at Royce and casually asked, "How was the inn? Meet any interesting people?"

"The inn was terrific!" he replied. "As far as meeting people, yes, I did. It seems like every person I have met on Antigua has been the exact person I needed to meet at just the right time."

Julian nodded. "Strange how that works, huh? Sir Godfrey used to tell me the same thing. Ever since then, I have noticed the same 'coincidental meetings' happening quite often in my own life."

Royce chuckled. "Don't I know it, Julian. Don't I know it. . ."

The two continued talking, enjoying the drive, and before they knew it, they had arrived at the dock at English Harbour.

"Well, this is about as far as I can get you, Royce. Sir Godfrey left me a key to the boat a few years ago, just in case it was ever needed. Seems like today may be one of those days!" He took a silver key off his key chain and tossed it to Royce. Pointing to the small craft, Julian added, "It will get you to the island quickly. It's fully gassed up—I checked it a couple of days ago—and there are life vests under the front seat."

Royce stepped out of the cab, thanked Julian, and added, "See you in a few hours . . . ?"

Julian chided him with a mischievous grin, "I think you know by now I'll be a step ahead of you."

Both men laughed, and Royce walked over to the waiting watercraft, jumped in, and fired up the engine.

"Like riding a bicycle," Royce said to himself with a nervous laugh.

Fortunately, it was an easy jaunt to the island, and when he reached the rickety little Redonda pier, it was clear where to dock the boat. Royce tied the vessel up, stepped out, and started toward the only structure on the tiny atoll: the Redonda lighthouse.

Royce began walking up the steep, narrow rocky path that led from the dock to the lighthouse, and as he finally approached the red-and-white-striped beacon, he heard someone call out in a British accent, "Hello there, can I help you?"

Royce surveyed his surroundings and didn't see anyone, but then he looked up at the top of the structure and saw a man who, from a distance, appeared to be around eighty years old, sticking his head out the window in curiosity.

Royce shouted up to him, "Hi! I'm looking for a gentleman named Thomas Langford. I'm a friend of Sir Godfrey Tillman."

The older man laughed and seemed to let down his guard. "Well, I don't know how much of a 'gentleman' I am, but I do try—and I definitely knew Sir Godfrey!

The door is unlocked, so come on up. I would come down and get you, but these days, I like to limit the times I go up and down the bloody stairs."

Royce smiled. "Perfect. I'll be right up!" He took a few more steps to the door, opened it slowly, then began walking up the long, winding staircase to the top. He surmised there were at least one hundred stairs, and after about fifty, he mumbled under his breath, "Good grief! 'Bloody stairs' for sure!"

After some huffing and puffing and multiple stops to rest along the way, Royce reached the top of the staircase and found Thomas Langford waiting for him.

"Good heavens, man," Thomas said in his deep British accent, "I thought you had gotten lost along the way." He laughed.

"Yeah, well, at about stair seventy-five, I started to yell for reinforcements, but here I am." Royce laughed and stuck out his hand. "I'm Royce Holloway."

The gentleman smiled and shook Royce's hand. "Mr. Holloway, it's a pleasure. I'm Thomas Langford, but please, call me Tom. Come in and make yourself comfortable."

"Nice to meet you, Tom." Royce looked around the large room, which was tastefully adorned in simple, classic decor. Smiling, he walked over and stood next to the large window overlooking the water, with Tom right behind him. Royce turned to him and offered, "Pretty much everything a man could need up here—including lots of solitude."

Tom smiled. "Oh, there's plenty of that, for sure. Has been for many years. Redonda Island was a little paradise of birds and endemic wildlife early on, but then in the eighteen hundreds, the British government realized there was a treasure trove of phosphate here to be used for making gunpowder, which brought in lots of miners—who also brought a lot of goats, oddly enough. Believe it or not, at one point, there was a nice little town here, including a local post office. Unfortunately, the people all left out of fear of an enemy invasion during World War I, but the bloody beasts remained, and have since multiplied. They've slowly eaten all the vegetation, until now the island has become a virtual moonscape—and I'm the only resident left. A few more years, and it will be uninhabitable, I'm afraid. Still, I do like the quiet."

"I had no idea," Royce said with surprise. "Until recently, I had never even heard of this island."

"Most folks haven't," Thomas responded with a grin. "It's like my own private isle." He gestured toward an attractive blue-and-beige couch. "Have a seat."

Royce nodded and sat down. "A beautiful piece of furniture," he commented. "And quite comfortable."

Mr. Langford gently added, "It was one of my wife's last purchases before she passed away about ten years ago. It's held up quite nicely, and I still think of her whenever I see it."

"I'm sorry for your loss," Royce quietly replied.

The gentleman nodded. "Thank you. Now, how can I be of help? You apparently knew my friend Godfrey. May I ask how you knew him?"

Royce shared with Thomas about the time he and Godfrey spent together at Jekyll, and what an impact it had made on Royce. "It didn't take long before I knew this was a special man—a special man indeed."

Thomas smiled and agreed. "God rest his soul! What a great man Godfrey Tillman was." He appeared to become a bit emotional, but quickly attempted to regroup and added, "Godfrey made me promise to celebrate, not mourn for him when the time came. I suppose most folks have been able to do that, but . . . I must admit, I have struggled since I heard the news. He was my best friend."

Royce paused. Then after what seemed like minutes, although it was only a few seconds, he said, "How did you come to know him?"

Thomas looked pensively out over the ocean, then slowly started to speak. "My wife and I took on this job over fifty years ago. We moved here from Birmingham—which is the second largest city in the United Kingdom—and we both wanted to get away from the noise and traffic and . . . well, civilization, I guess you could say." He smiled. "It was the perfect fit for us. I always loved my wife, of course, but the sea was a close second, as I had been a sailor for many years. But when Margaret passed away, even as much as I loved the sea and the lighthouse, I became lonely and depressed. I'm one of the last lighthouse keepers in the world, and when I'm gone, the government has said there will be no replacement for me or my position. I could see the writing on the wall, and I began thinking, 'Maybe it's time. . .'"His voice faded.

In genuine Royce Holloway style, he leaned in and gently encouraged the man to continue with his heartfelt sentiments.

Tom smiled appreciatively. "One day, when I felt as if I was at my breaking point, I received a call from Sir Godfrey. He told me he had heard there was a fellow Brit manning the lighthouse, and he wanted to meet me—especially since he was living close by."

Royce nodded as the older gentleman continued his story.

"I offered for him to come over, which he did that same day. When Godfrey arrived, I felt as if the weight of the world had been lifted off me. We hit it off immediately. He listened to me, and I was grateful for the companionship—especially since he was from the UK, and we had much in common. But not only that, Sir Godfrey felt *he* could open up to *me*—as a friend. He knew his knighthood was something that people were impressed by, and they usually wanted to know how he did it. But to me, he was just Godfrey. We never talked about his success in business or his relationships with people in the British government—unless it was something *he* wanted to share."

"How wonderful that you both had each other. True friendship is a gift, indeed," Royce quietly said. "You must miss him."

"Very much so," Thomas replied softly. "Godfrey would share things here that he wouldn't share with anyone else—and I was the same way with him. It's a rare honor to have someone like that in your life."

"Yes," Royce agreed. "Even a man who seems larger than life, like Godfrey, is simply a person with hopes and dreams and a need for friendship. Plus, I'm sure he had his flaws, like we all do."

Thomas nodded slowly. "It's true, Royce, and I'm sure Godfrey would have wanted you to know that. He had flaws like all of us do. Just because we make mistakes—even big ones—doesn't mean we can't still impact the world in a mighty way. Godfrey often said, 'Most often, we are even better people *because* of those perceived mistakes or failures. But we must give ourselves permission to extract the lessons from the pain, put the ghosts of the past behind us, and go on.'"

Royce paused for a moment, taking in those impactful words. "That's a powerful and freeing concept you just shared," Royce commented thoughtfully. "I wish I had understood it many years ago, as I would have saved myself a lot of self-inflicted suffering."

Thomas smiled and nodded in an understanding way. "Believe me, Royce, I understand. For some reason, after my wife passed away, I began beating myself up more and more, thinking about what I wished I had done differently. I played the 'if only' game for so long. Now I know that not only is that something she would not have wanted me to do, but I also wasted a lot of time that could have been applied to helping others live in a happier, more fulfilled way. Today, my life is dedicated to living gratefully in the present and being thankful for the lessons learned along the way."

"Wise words, Tom," Royce replied. "Sounds like something our friend Godfrey would approve of." He winked, and the older gentleman smiled appreciatively.

Thomas then added, "Speaking of our friend Godfrey . . . the last time he came to visit, he asked me to hold onto something for someone special. He said I would know who the recipient should be when the time came—and now I know what he meant." He smiled broadly.

Oddly enough, even though this entire "treasure hunt" had been so utterly fascinating and engaging, Royce had found himself getting used to his meetings habitually ending with a mystery envelope left for him by Godfrey. He watched as Thomas Langford stood up, walked over to a gold-framed painting on the wall, and began staring at it. It was a scene of a beautiful, towering old lighthouse made of gorgeous brown stone. The sky was a brilliant blue, with a few wispy white clouds hanging in the air, and two white seagulls hovered just over the top of the beacon.

As if speaking to the wall, Thomas didn't turn around as he began, "It's the Tower of Hercules in Spain—the oldest lighthouse in the world. They say it was built in the first century AD. When Margaret and I saw the lighthouse on a visit to that country, we were both in awe. We returned home and had this painting commissioned, as it was that visit which made us realize we wanted to be lighthouse keepers." Thomas's voice cracked as he added, "The seagulls represented the two of us, flying free to a new life together. . ."

"I'm sorry, Thomas," Royce compassionately replied.

With typical British composure, Thomas stood up straight and commented, "As I said, it's time now to live in the present, not the past." At that point, he reached up and swiftly took the painting off the wall.

Not understanding, Royce cried out, "Wait! Thomas, what—"

It was then that Royce noticed the outline of an apparent medium-sized combination safe behind the place where the painting had hung, with a dial protruding shallowly from the wall. Without even acknowledging Royce's outburst, Thomas began delicately turning the tumbler, entering the precise combination. Royce was mesmerized as Thomas gently twisted the knob one last time to the left, and the safe door opened. He reached inside and pulled out an item about the size of a shoebox, wrapped in brown butcher paper and secured by a neatly tied string.

Turning away from the safe and reaching out to hand Royce the package, Thomas smiled as he noted the younger man's awestruck look.

"I've been holding it for Godfrey for quite some time, but I don't know what it is. Godfrey would have told me, but I got the distinct impression that this was something incredibly special, and I didn't want him to feel like he had to share the story with me, so I didn't ask questions. I simply accepted it from him and promised to keep it safe, and it has never been touched since the day he delivered it and I placed it in the safe."

"A true friend. You are an amazing man, Thomas," Royce said with a look of admiration.

"It was the least I could do, given all Godfrey had done for me. If you wish, I'll leave you for a few minutes while you open it."

Royce nodded and smiled. "Thank you."

As Thomas exited the room, Royce looked down at the package he was now holding. With trembling hands, he slowly and cautiously opened it, and with tears welling up in his eyes, he gradually made out the contents of the bundle: a weathered copy of *The Six Principles of Sacred Power*. He carefully opened the book, and inside the cover was a signature, written in Hindi. Royce had seen it on historical Indian documents he had studied in the past, and he knew immediately what it was.

It was the signature of Mohandas K. Gandhi.

Royce leaned back, looked at the ceiling, and exhaled. The search was over. He was holding in his hands one of the most valuable antiquities in the world—and as elated as he felt, he was also . . . terrified. Thoughts raced through his mind. *What do I do with it? How do I handle it? Where should I keep it? Should I insure it . . . ?*

Right then, Royce noticed an envelope sticking out just above the back page of the book. He gently removed it, opened it, and eagerly began reading:

Dear Royce,

Ah, yes, your determination has finally paid off! As you know, the book now in your possession is one that has changed the world. Your unshakable patience and persistence in finding it are representative of the kind of supreme powers we all have available to us, as The Six Principles of Sacred Power *makes clear. Well done.*

I have often imagined what Mr. Gandhi's emotions must have been while writing the book, as he uncovered each of the universal lessons of the spiritual masters. Finding every new principle must have been like unearthing an invaluable nugget of pure gold from years of hiding in a deep, dark mine.

I'll bet it felt a lot like what you are feeling now—and rightfully so.

You are surely wondering what to do next. Well, as you can guess, my answer is the same: 'Simply allow the answer to unfold'—which I think you have gotten quite good at by now.

I would, however, make one suggestion. You are now close to my home in Shirley Heights. Return there for the evening and see what may aid you in the next steps of your journey. I have a feeling you will find what you need.

For me, my good man, I will now leave you to carry on. You are well prepared—more so than ever, I would suspect—to bring light to a world that is much in need of it.

I am beyond grateful that our paths crossed, and I wholeheartedly trust that all will continue to go according to God's great plan for your life—and for humanity.

Namaste, my friend,

Godfrey

Fifteen minutes had passed in a blink, and suddenly Royce's thoughts were interrupted by Thomas gently calling to him from the next room, "All good, my friend?"

Royce tenderly wrapped the book back up, placed the envelope and letter back inside it, and stood up, calling back to Thomas, "Yes, thank you. Come in."

As the older man entered the room, Royce stepped forward. "I'm so thankful you kept this for Sir Godfrey. I know his trust in you meant the world to him."

Still unaware of the contents of the package, Thomas replied, "Godfrey and I trusted each other with our lives, Royce. For him to feel the need to shield me from this, I know it must have been for my own good. I am honored to have been able to be of service to him—and to you."

Royce smiled and reached out to shake Thomas's hand. "Thank you, sir—and now I guess it's time for me to be on my way. I've got a little homework Godfrey left me with, so I'd better get to it."

"Homework, eh? Well, I understand," the older man said with a grin as he clasped Royce's hand. "When it came to productivity, Godfrey didn't want the grass to grow under his feet, or anyone else's feet in his circle."

The two men laughed heartily.

Royce turned and walked out the door, down the long staircase, and out to the little boat waiting for him at the dock. Stepping in cautiously, he placed his delicate package in a compartment near the craft's dashboard, then quickly strapped on his life jacket. Starting the boat's engine, Royce thought about Godfrey's written words: "I have a feeling you will find what you need."

As he edged the boat away from the dock and out into the vast, blue Caribbean Sea, a chill suddenly went up his spine as he wondered what those words would come to mean. . .

CHAPTER 16

With Royce consumed by eagerness and the uncertainty of what lay ahead, the short boat ride back to the mainland seemed to take forever. But once he arrived at his destination, he glanced at his watch and saw it had only been fifteen minutes since he left the landing at Redonda.

Royce smoothly navigated the craft to its resting place and shut off the engine. Removing his life vest, he grabbed his precious cargo from the compartment and exited the boat, then tied it securely to the mooring. Stepping up onto the dock, he looked off in the distance and saw Julian standing outside the cab, leaning against the driver's side window with his arms crossed.

Once Royce got within earshot, the young man yelled with a laugh, "Hey, boss, I thought you would never make it back!"

"Yeah, yeah, I know. . . I was a little, um, busy, I guess you could say." Royce grinned.

"Ok, we'll leave it at that," Julian said good-naturedly. "Where to now?"

"I'm going to make it easy for you, my friend. This will be my last trip; I just need to go back to Sir Godfrey's place."

"Oh, wow, you *are* being kind. Jump in!" he said with a smile.

It was only a few minutes before Godfrey's house came into view. Julian pulled up to the gate and put in the code he knew so well, then when the gate opened, he slowly drove the vehicle toward the home.

"Looks like Suzanne got herself a new car," the young cabbie offered in jest upon seeing a black limousine inexplicably parked out front.

"Odd," Royce replied with a note of perplexity. "Then again, it may be someone coming to pay their respects. Could be a number of people."

Pulling up next to the limo, Julian looked at his American passenger and said, "I'm going to miss you, Royce. Our time together reminded me of my time with Sir Godfrey. For some reason, you two seem to be a lot alike."

Royce smiled. "I consider that the ultimate compliment, Julian."

Picking up his travel bag, Royce then reached into his pocket, pulled out a large wad of fifty-dollar bills, and handed it gently to Julian. "This should take care of all the trips you've escorted me on, old buddy."

Julian looked at the huge payment with wide eyes and exclaimed, "Royce there must be a thousand dollars here!"

Royce smiled. "Well deserved, I would say. Now take care, Julian. I won't forget you." Royce appreciatively shook the young man's hand, closed the taxi door, and walked up to the entrance of Godfrey's home.

Knocking several times, Royce heard Suzanne's cheerful voice. "Coming!"

When she opened the door, although Suzanne was happy to see Royce, she didn't seem surprised by his sudden appearance. In fact, it was almost as if she had been expecting him—which struck him as odd. After a welcoming embrace, she said excitedly, "Royce, I can't wait to hear about your journey—you must have so much to share. Do come in!"

Royce entered and looked around, expecting to see guests in the home.

"Looking for someone?" Suzanne asked with a grin.

"Well, um, I saw the shiny black limo outside, and I thought maybe you had a VIP here or something." Royce smiled.

"VIP? Certainly not—aside from you." She grinned again. "Well, there is *one* special guest who just recently arrived. In fact, I think you may know them."

Royce shrugged and waited for a clue.

Suzanne looked at Royce calmly, then motioned behind her to the left, toward the office.

As Royce's gaze followed Suzanne's gesture, a figure slowly emerged and began walking toward Royce as he stared in disbelief. . .

"Maya!"

A broad smile spread across the woman's face as she stepped into full view. "Hello Royce."

Tears rolled down Royce's face as he ran over and put his arms around her in a tender, nostalgic way.

At that moment, Royce glanced over Maya's shoulder and saw a large, muscular Indian man standing behind her, at full attention, just inside the office door. As Royce pulled gently away, he laughed. "I'm guessing this is your, um, escort."

She flashed that same carefree smile Royce remembered so well. "Well, I've learned the hard way that one can't be too safe these days, if you know what I mean."

Maya then turned and waved the man forward. "This is Royce Holloway, my good friend from America. Royce, this is Ramesh, my driver and personal bodyguard from India."

"Nice to meet you," Royce replied as he extended his hand and smiled.

The burly man mustered a quick smile and shook Royce's outstretched hand.

Maya looked at Royce, then at Suzanne, and asked them both to sit down.

Gazing at the noble Indian woman, Royce noticed how she seemed to not have changed at all over the five years since he had last seen her. Her multicolored pastel sari fit her shapely figure perfectly, and her long hair was still dark and shiny. The two gold hoop earrings she wore nicely accented her soft, brown skin.

"Maya . . . when did you get here—and *what* are you doing here?" Royce managed.

As if she hadn't heard him, Maya slowly turned away, taking in their surroundings, then quickly turned back to address Royce. "Forgive my distraction, Royce. I was never able to come and visit Sir Godfrey while he lived here. This home is magnificent." She then turned to Suzanne and added with a smile, "I understand the impeccability and beauty of the home is in great part due to all your hard work, Suzanne. Well done."

Suzanne replied humbly, "Thank you, Maya. It has been an honor."

Maya then looked at Ramesh and Suzanne and politely asked, "Would you two kindly allow me a few moments with Royce?"

They nodded. Suzanne stood up and walked into the kitchen as Ramesh dutifully exited into the office.

Maya then turned back to Royce and replied, "Now I will answer your question—or should I say 'questions,' which you still seem to have no shortage of after all these years!"

The two laughed as they thought back to those times in her Georgia gardens all those years ago.

Royce grimaced playfully, then smiled. "I know, I know. . . But at least now my questions are questions of interest and not just curiosity."

Maya shook her head and smiled. "Hmmm, if you say so. So, as far as *when* I arrived, it was last night, and Suzanne was kind enough to allow us to stay in this lovely place. She and I had some wonderful conversation. As far as *why* I'm here, well, that's a little more involved."

Royce raised a deeply inquisitive eyebrow.

"This is a quick first stop on a two-week trip. I will be leaving Antigua early this evening to catch a flight to the next islands south of here—the country of Trinidad and Tobago. I will leave from there in a few days and go to northern South America—first to Guyana, then over the border to Suriname, before going back to India."

Royce thought for a moment. "All of those countries have large Hindu populations. Is this a business trip?"

Maya nodded and smiled. "I see your knowledge of other nations and their people is still keen. Yes, all those countries are home to influential Indian people who continue to support the movement I have been part of in the north of India. I'm going to visit those stakeholders and thank them personally for their confidence and their support of me and the party."

Royce shook his head and said, "The Caribbean and South America? Maya, that's quite a journey from India! I think you must know people everywhere in the world."

Maya smiled, then gently guided the conversation on a different course. "Royce, I understand that you, too, have been on quite a journey over the last few days. In fact, your quest is the reason I began my trip by stopping in Antigua."

Royce quickly wondered aloud, "How did you know?"

Maya paused briefly, then leaned forward slightly. "I knew Sir Godfrey had Mr. Gandhi's book in safekeeping, and I also understood that he was going to pass it on to you."

Royce's head was spinning. "What? But how? And I also can't understand . . . how was he able to write each of those letters directly to *me*, when I just met him at Jekyll Island last week?

Maya smiled. "When people have a relationship based on common experiences at the level Sir Godfrey and I did, the trust created is unequivocal. Many months ago, he asked who I believed would be a proper steward of Mr. Gandhi's book. When I shared with him that I believed *you* would be the perfect candidate, Godfrey immediately and implicitly agreed. In fact, he smiled, and his precise words were, 'That's who I was hoping you might suggest.' Shortly after that, before he left on his trip, he wrote and then handed out the various letters you received on your journey."

"You mean he wrote those letters before he even *knew* me—and before he even knew he was going to meet me?" Royce asked with a look of disbelief.

Maya looked directly into his eyes and said calmly, "In a way, he knew you before he knew you, Royce—and he also fully believed your paths would cross at the perfect time. In the same way that the right teachers arrive punctually, so do the correct students."

With humility, Royce replied quietly, "Thank you, Maya."

Maya smiled. "The book you have found is, as you know, something that the world can only imagine exists. But . . . there is more to this than just finding the book, Royce. Much more."

Now even more perplexed, Royce leaned back, wrinkled his forehead, and rubbed his chin.

Maya went on, "When Godfrey met you at Jekyll Island, he knew you were ready to learn the Four Daily Pillars of Wisdom—and I am aware that you learned the lessons very well. Yet he also wisely knew for you to be fully prepared for the steep path of spiritual mastery ahead, you needed to be given an opportunity to apply what you had learned—at an exceptionally high level. This mission he created for you was exactly that."

"I . . . I don't even know what to say," Royce stammered.

Maya smiled and continued, "The diverse individuals you met over these last few days provided practical examples of how seemingly 'ordinary' people can rise above incredible hardships to do *extraordinary* things. As you saw, Godfrey's encouragement gave each of them newfound faith in their abilities. Although some people might think differently, it isn't magic; their results stemmed from tapping into the power we all have, which is typically buried underneath layers of anxiety, doubt, and fear, as *The Six Principles of Sacred Power* teaches us."

Royce nodded in agreement and then added, "Plus, not only did the lessons change *them*, but what they learned consequently inspired them to change the lives of others. It's the great ripple effect of goodness you and I talked about in the gardens."

"Correct," Maya affirmed with a smile. "And you needed to experience it this way, and at this pragmatic level, to see the *astounding* potential every one of us has for changing the world—regardless of race, gender, social status, age, or any other factor."

Royce stammered, "So, meeting all those people I met, and finally being led to Mr. Gandhi's personal book, was . . . a test?"

"More like a final confirmation, or a living dissertation before the ultimate graduation, I would say," Maya quipped with a grin.

"Well, I hope I passed," Royce responded with a nervous laugh.

"You passed beautifully." Maya beamed.

"Ok, but Maya, there's still something I don't understand. . ."

Maya looked patiently at Royce, as if she knew what was coming next.

"One of the last things Godfrey said to me on Jekyll was that there was a person I needed to meet here on Antigua. Who *was* the one person I was supposed to meet? Was it one of the people along the way—or even Julian, the taxi driver?" He paused, then slowly said, "Or Maya . . . are *you* the one I was supposed to meet?"

Maya smiled and shook her head gently. "Royce, the person you needed to meet was . . . *you*."

"Me?" he repeated incredulously.

"Yes, Royce. You needed to viscerally understand the connection we all have in this life. We are all so similar, even though we all *seem* so different. Each of those people you met—Dianne, Giff, Elizabeth, Roberto, Thomas, and yes, even Oswaldo and Julian—have experienced life situations and subsequent solutions you could somehow relate to. In a way, each person you met *was* you."

Royce's blank look encouraged Maya to continue.

"This was an indoctrination into a new degree of compassionate understanding of human nature. Sympathy is feeling *for* people, which most can easily do. But empathy is feeling *with* people. It arises from a deep, benevolent understanding of others, and it is a level of compassion most people are not as familiar with. Now more than ever, after this experience, you understand how and why empathy is so important in connecting with and positively affecting peoples' lives. As you likely gleaned from the people you met, Sir Godfrey had a gift for relating to people in this way."

Royce again shook his head in amazement. As he thought back over the last few days, he now understood the reason he had felt such a kinship with each of the people on his journey.

Before Royce could speak, Maya added, "Yes, it is no wonder you felt you had something in common with each of them, because you were essentially looking in the mirror—the mirror of life."

"Now that I understand this, I've got to go back and talk with them all!" said Royce excitedly. "There must be so much more I can learn from them, and deeper ways I can relate to each of them. . ."

Maya smiled and softly shook her head. "The lessons are complete, Royce. There is no going back."

Royce had a look of disbelief. "Maya, are you saying they would be *gone* if I went back to find them?"

"Maybe. Maybe not," Maya said neutrally. "Royce, as you know, lessons and teachers appear when you're ready, and fade away once you learn those lessons. You have learned the lessons you were meant to learn in Antigua."

Maya saw a look of disappointment cross Royce's face. She continued, "Rest assured, Royce, new mentors will arrive in their own ways when you need them in the future." She smiled.

Royce seemed to be slowly coming to terms with Maya's explanation. "But did they know they were teaching me?" he wondered aloud.

Maya shrugged. "Possibly. I'm not sure. It's a valuable reminder, however, that we are always teaching one another through our words and actions, whether we know our 'students' are paying attention or not."

Royce nodded, listening intently.

She added, "Royce, on this journey, you have been exposed to the ultimate lesson. It's one that every pilgrim on this road to mastery must eventually come face to face with, and then be willing to take on in their own way."

Royce leaned forward, listening with everything he had in his being.

"Our mission is to peacefully and powerfully live out our values such that, regardless of any outward differences we might have with them, people will see the strength and compassion of God in us, and believe that they, too, have the same spark within them, which can be fanned into a flame that can change the world." Maya concluded gently, "It's the narrow path of the spiritual warrior, Royce."

Maya took a minute to let all this sink in.

Royce was clearly captivated by her words. After several seconds, as if a light bulb had just gone off in his head, he replied, "It makes total sense now. We *are* all connected, Maya—whether we're willing to admit it or not. And as you said, though most people may believe the difference between empathy and sympathy is subtle, I now understand it at a new level. When one has sympathy, yes, they feel for the other person. But when one has *empathy*, it can—if used properly—transfer energy, courage, and strength to the other person. Those kinds of interactions empower the giver *and* the receiver, or the teacher and the student. In fact, at that supreme level of compassion, the line between them is probably difficult to distinguish."

Maya smiled and softly touched Royce's cheek. "Ah, yes, my student has once again learned well. I am proud of you, Royce."

Royce felt himself blushing. "Thank you, Maya. After all this time, your words still mean so much to me."

He paused, then looked down at the small travel bag he had set securely beside him. Reaching inside, he carefully grasped and unwrapped the copy of *The Six Principles of Sacred Power* and held it up for Maya to see.

Maya gazed in awe at the weathered manuscript, and her eyes became misty as Royce gently handed it to her.

"Mahatma's personal copy," she whispered reverently as she slowly reached out and accepted it. Opening the book, she turned to the inscribed page, then looked up at Royce in amazement. "I can't believe it."

Royce smiled. "I think *you* are the correct person to be the keeper of this treasure, Maya. I know you'll find the exact right place for it. *My* treasure can be found in the lessons I learned from those extraordinary mentors over the last three days—lessons I will carry with me forever."

Maya was clearly moved by the gesture. As she fought back tears, she gently replied, "Royce, I would be both honored and humbled to do so. I assure you this precious relic will be well taken care of."

Royce nodded and said with a grin, "I have no doubt of that."

Just then, Ramesh entered the room and nervously interjected, "Maya, forgive me, but time is getting away from us. The flight from St. John's to Port of Spain is short, but we still need to get to the airport early, and you have back-to-back appointments with the government officials there. We should go, ma'am."

About that same time, Suzanne walked in and saw the group gathering their possessions. "Maya, must you leave so soon?" she asked.

With a soft smile, Maya looked at Royce and then turned back to Suzanne. "Yes, it's time. I think my work is done here, and I'm sure Royce has lots to tell you about his adventures over the last few days."

Royce smiled broadly. "Well, I guess I *could* hang around a little bit longer. I've been craving some homemade banana bread lately—and I wouldn't mind another day in paradise!"

Suzanne laughed as Royce then walked over to Maya, with Ramesh looking anxiously at his watch as he walked briskly past her out to the limousine.

"Maya, to see you again is a gift among gifts. I only wish our time together could have been longer; I've missed you and our conversations so much." He hugged her tightly, then pulling slowly away, he looked into her eyes and quietly said, "Goodbye, my dear mentor. Until we meet again—wherever and whenever that will be."

Maya smiled and nodded calmly and approvingly, then turned and began walking toward the door, held open for her by Suzanne. Reaching the threshold, Maya thanked Suzanne for her hospitality, then looked back at Royce and offered with a tone of intrigue, "By the way, Royce, I'll be in touch when I return to India. I have a strong intuition our next meeting may be sooner than you might think."

Taking note of Royce's deeply puzzled look, Maya simply smiled, turned away, and gracefully walked into the warm, breezy Caribbean evening.

Find more inspirational stories at
www.skipjohnsonauthor.com

ABOUT SKIP JOHNSON

Skip Johnson is an award-winning inspirational author whose goal is to empower, inspire, and enrich the lives of his readers.

He is known for his easy-going style of adventurous storytelling, with rich elements of spirituality, mysticism, and personal growth woven throughout his books. One prominent aspect of Skip's writing is how he takes readers on symbolic journeys of self-discovery and enlightenment. His characters often find themselves on treks to faraway places where meetings with wise mystical mentors lead readers to contemplate their own personal and spiritual journeys and how their lives can be more fulfilling and joyful.

His storytelling is simple yet profound, allowing readers from all walks of life to extract and quickly apply the nuggets of wisdom, compassion, and peacefulness that permeate the pages of his narratives. He uses crystal-clear imagery to create the feeling for readers of being right beside each character on their life-changing, heroic journey in every saga.

Skip's books are both spiritual and practical. Each story encourages readers to look inside themselves for the magic, courage, and strength that is often deeply hidden within themselves, patiently waiting to be released to powerfully impact the world.

Based in Georgia, Skip himself has traveled many paths, including that of a motivational speaker, a business leader, a master tennis professional, and a world traveler. These experiences have shaped his writing, and the wisdom and insights woven into each story leave readers filled with wonder, gratitude, and enthusiasm for the days ahead.

His works have earned various award designations, including the Maxy Awards Book of the Year, the International Book Award, and the Nautilus Silver Winner Award.

To see all of Skip's books and free e-books, visit https://www.skipjohnsonauthor.com/.

CAN I ASK A FAVOR?

Thank you for reading my book! Would you do me a favor and take a moment to write a short review on Amazon? Reviews are so important to authors like me, and if you would share your thoughts so others can find out about my writing, I would be truly grateful.

If you leave a review, feel free to let me know by dropping me an email at:

skipjohnsonauthor1@gmail.com
so I can thank you personally!

www.ingramcontent.com/pod-product-compliance
Lightning Source LLC
Chambersburg PA
CBHW070851050426
42453CB00012B/2143